The *Charity*
TRUSTEE'S
HANDBOOK

D1325229

Mike Eastwood

DIRECTORY OF SOCIAL CHANGE

CAF

Published by
Directory of Social Change
24 Stephenson Way
London NW1 2DP
Tel. 020 7209 5151; Fax: 020 7391 4804
e-mail: books@dsc.org.uk
from whom further copies and a full books catalogue are available.

Directory of Social Change is a Registered Charity no. 800517

First published 2001
Reprinted 2003

ISBN 1 900360 88 8

British Library Cataloguing in Publication Data
A catalogue record for this book is available from the British Library

Text and cover designed by Sarah Nicholson

Typeset, printed and bound by Stephen Austin, Hertford

Other Directory of Social Change departments in London:
Courses and conferences tel: 020 7209 4949
Charity Centre tel: 020 7209 1015
Charityfair tel: 020 7391 4848
Publicity and Web Content tel: 020 7391 4900
Publicity and research tel: 020 7391 4880

Directory of Social Change Northern Office:
Federation House, Hope Street, Liverpool L1 9BW
Courses and conferences tel: 0151 708 0117
Policy and Research tel: 0151 708 0136

Contents

For Nikki, Beth, Jessica and Ben

About the series

Series editor: Alison Baxter

This book is the first in a series of starter guides aimed primarily at those who are new to the voluntary sector. The series is designed for people involved with charities or voluntary organisations or community groups of any size. All the titles offer practical, straightforward advice to enable readers to get the most out of their roles and responsibilities.

Other guides will cover areas such as fundraising, the role of the charity treasurer, and minute taking.

For further information, please contact the Directory of Social Change (see page 106 for details).

Introduction

There are probably about a million people currently serving as charity trustees in the UK. They range from people sitting on trustee boards of household-name charities, such as Oxfam and the National Trust, to members of the management committees of small, local charities operating in a single village or parish. They include members of church councils, some housing associations, Parent–Teacher Associations and community groups, and even some school governors.

This is a book for those who are, or are thinking of becoming, a charity trustee. It doesn't aim to tell you everything; rather, it aims to give you enough information to decide whether you should become a trustee or, if you are already one, some ideas on how to make your trusteeship more rewarding. Although it refers particularly to charities, it will also be useful for committee members of other community and voluntary organisations that are not registered charities.

It can be read straight through from start to finish. However, you can also use it as a basic reference guide and dip into it to help you with particular issues or concerns.

Being a trustee is, or should be, fulfilling. You are using your skills to help an organisation that you believe in to change things for the better. Sometimes this can be frustrating; often it can be challenging; occasionally you will want to give the whole thing up. However, fundamentally you should derive a lot of personal satisfaction from seeing something you are committed to flourish and develop.

Good luck!

Acknowledgements

The author and publishers would like to thank Tim Cook, Ruth Froggatt and Lucy Swanson for reading through various drafts of this book, providing helpful comments and valuable insights.

Thanks, too, to Sandy Adirondack for the helpful checklists at the back of the book.

And thanks to the many trustees and management committee members who have shared their experiences with us.

PART **ONE**

What makes a good trustee?

1 What is a trustee?

This is not a book mainly about charity law, nor about the details of your legal responsibilities and liabilities. Rather, it aims to be a practical guide about how to operate effectively as a trustee. For information on legal issues, see *Charitable Status* (details on page 115). However, it is important to start by answering two basic questions: 'What is a trustee?' and 'What are you letting yourself in for when you become a trustee?'

First, by becoming a trustee, you are joining the voluntary sector. There are currently over 180,000 registered charities in the UK, each with its own board of trustees, with a combined annual income of around £14 billion. They cover an enormous range of activities, from the arts to the environment, from health to welfare, from educating pre-school children to caring for older people in poor health, from maintaining the nation's heritage to providing accommodation for homeless people.

❝ The most rewarding thing about being a trustee is seeing things happen in the community. **❞**

Voluntary organisations are not the only ones working in these areas. Government and the private sector are also active here, providing services targeting individuals and their communities. However, there are clear differences in how voluntary organisations do things compared with the public and private sectors. For example:

- Voluntary organisations do not make profits; any surpluses at the end of the year are ploughed back into the work of the charity rather than distributed to shareholders.
- Compared with the government and corporate sectors, this 'third sector' of voluntary organisations is tiny. The annual turnover of BT is bigger than the entire voluntary sector; Oxfam's income is about one per cent of that of an ailing Marks & Spencer; all the health charities combined could probably keep the National Health Service going for about a fortnight. In fact, most registered charities in the UK have an annual income of under £20,000.
- Voluntary organisations are not under the control of politicians or political appointees. Government cannot require them to undertake or discontinue particular activities.

- Many voluntary organisations rely heavily on volunteers to do their work. It is estimated that over 20 million people a year will do some voluntary work for a charity or voluntary organisation.

This is by no means an exhaustive list. However, it does illustrate the point that voluntary organisations have a particular role to play in society. They cannot replace government; their motivations are different from those in the private sector; people view them differently from other sectors (how many people would willingly do unpaid work for their local bank or the local JobCentre?). And it is up to the trustees to define the particular role that their charity will play.

Trustees are also responsible, accountable and liable for the actions of their charity. One of the more sobering aspects of being a trustee is that you are a member of the group that will take the rap if anything goes seriously wrong. For example, if a charity does not have enough money to pay its bills this is deemed to be the responsibility of its trustees rather than its staff. Similarly, if a charity oversteps its constitutional boundaries (for example, if it provides services outside its permitted geographical area), such activities are illegal and the trustees will be held to account. The responsibilities and liabilities of trustees are a serious matter. The key ones are outlined later in this chapter, although you might also want to read up more fully on them elsewhere (the Charity Commission produces a series of useful guides – see page 112 for details).

So what, or who, is a trustee? Technically, charity trustees are the people who, according to the charity's constitution or governing document, are responsible for controlling the management and administration of the charity. Trustees may also be called management committee members, governors, council members or executive committee members. It doesn't matter what you are called; it is the function you have that determines whether or not you are a trustee.

We generally use the term 'management committee member' rather than 'trustee' in this book. This is because most voluntary organisations tend to refer to 'the management committee' rather than 'the trustees'. But even if the title varies, the role and legal status are the same.

Completing Checklist 1, *The legal and management framework* (see page 89), will help you to think through the way that your management committee operates.

In practice, are you a full voting member of the management committee of your charity? And is your charity an independent body, with its own constitution? If so, you are a charity trustee.

Key concept – governance

It is often said that the trustees' key function is one of **governance** rather than **management**.

Governance is the process a management committee uses to make sure that the organisation operates effectively, that it has a clear mission and strategy. However, governance is not necessarily about doing the work; rather, it is about making sure that things are done. For example, it is about ensuring that an organisation is well managed, but not necessarily about managing it. It is about making sure that the organisation has clear aims and priorities, policies and procedures, but not necessarily about forming them. It is about making certain that the organisation has appropriate systems, but not necessarily about developing them. It is about ensuring that the organisation has sufficient resources (people, equipment, expertise, etc.), although not necessarily about providing them. And so on.

(You may find it useful to turn to Checklist 2, *Governance* – see page 90.)

Management is more about the day-to-day responsibilities of doing the work, delivering the services, appointing and supervising staff – in short, implementing trustee decisions.

So, for example, trustees should decide the amount of financial information they need to ensure that the organisation is progressing as planned; staff need to provide trustees with that information.

In practice, in smaller organisations, trustees may well be involved both in the planning, decision-making and monitoring work (governance), and also in actually doing some or most of the work (management). Even so, it is worth being aware of the distinction between the two responsibilities so that if the organisation grows, the management committee can focus more on the governance side and staff on management. Also, it will help you to keep management committee meetings focused on the bigger picture of governance, instead of them getting too bogged down in the urgency and detail of management.

What are the responsibilities of trustees?

Taking personal responsibility

As a management committee member you accept personal responsibility for the activities of your organisation. This personal responsibility is shared between you and the other committee members. You are expected to know and understand your role. Ignorance is no excuse.

You are generally considered to have supported the decisions made by committee members unless you can demonstrate your active opposition to them. Disagreeing at meetings before a consensus is reached is not enough. If you disagree on a matter of importance, your active and continued opposition should be recorded in the minutes. Even then, if you continue to serve as a management committee member you are generally held to be jointly responsible, including for a decision that you voted against.

Avoiding conflicts of interest

Charity trustees must act solely in the interests of their charity, irrespective of how they were appointed. For example, local councillors often sit on the management committees of local charities. However, they are not there to represent the local authority's interests and wishes; they, like their fellow trustees, should have the charity's best interests in mind. This applies equally to the management committee member who is also a beneficiary of the charity (and therefore stands personally to gain or lose from certain decisions) as to the trustee who is a friend or relative of someone tendering for a contract of work.

Management committee members should always try to avoid putting themselves in a position where their duty to act in the charity's best interests conflicts with their personal interests. If they cannot, they should declare this conflict of interest and usually withdraw from any further discussion on the matter.

Acting with care

At all times, you are expected to act reasonably, in the interests of your beneficiaries and with a high standard of care. 'Reasonably' is usually taken to mean what an ordinary person in that situation would consider reasonable. If you are a charity trustee, failing to act reasonably and with care may put you in breach of trust. This may make you personally liable for any debts or claims which result from your actions.

Keeping an eye on finances

You need to be particularly careful about finances. You must be satisfied that the organisation is in control of its financial planning (budgets) and monitoring (regular reports on progress, sometimes called management accounts), that forecasts are reasonable and that progress is assessed regularly. You also need to guard against fraud, and ensure that safeguards are in place regarding matters such as handling cash and opening the post.

The general rule is that if you see problems looming, act sooner rather than later; don't just hope that things will turn out all right. As mentioned above, you can become personally liable for the debts of your charity.

Obeying the law

You must make sure that legal requirements are met. The most important requirement is to make sure that the organisation works entirely towards fulfilling its objectives and works in accordance with its constitution. Any money given to you must be used for the declared charitable purposes of your organisation and also for any precise purposes for which it was given. Charity trustees could be asked to make good any money spent on projects which were outside the charitable purposes of their organisation.

It is easy to be intimidated by your responsibilities and possible liabilities. However, try to keep a balanced view. Use your responsibilities and liabilities to remind you and your fellow trustees to act carefully ('prudently' in legal terms), lawfully and in accordance with your constitution – but don't let them bog you down completely. Be particularly careful when entering into major contracts or borrowing large sums. If you get this wrong and you end up owing more money than the charity has, you will be in a potentially difficult legal situation and will need to seek professional advice. There are ways of limiting your personal liability, such as insuring against fraud or setting up a registered company, although these are not always appropriate for a small organisation. See *Charitable Status* for more on this – details on page 115.

Can trustees be paid for their trusteeship?

The answer to this question is almost always 'No'. You give your time willingly and not for personal gain. This is one reason why paid members of staff generally cannot (and should not) be trustees. They can attend trustee meetings if the committee so wishes; they can speak and advise; but they cannot vote.

You can claim for travel expenses and childcare costs incurred by attending trustee meetings and other trustee business; you can claim the cost of training courses and conferences connected with your trusteeship; you can even claim back the cost of buying this book. Basically, you can claim back any money that you pay out to fulfil your obligations as a trustee. However, it is difficult to claim for compensation for lost earnings while attending to trustee business. You should certainly not be paid an honorarium or annual retainer, however small. You are giving your time, enthusiasm, skills and commitment to something that you think is worthwhile – and you are giving them for free.

2 Who can be a trustee?

Legal requirements

There are certain legal requirements which govern who can be a trustee. You cannot be a trustee if you:

- are aged under 18 (unless the charity is a registered company);
- have been convicted of an offence involving dishonesty or deception, unless the conviction is regarded as 'spent' (i.e. there has been a set period of rehabilitation, during which time you have committed no further offence);
- are an undischarged bankrupt;
- have been previously removed from trusteeship of a charity by the court or the Charity Commission;
- are under a disqualification order under the Company Directors Disqualification Act 1986.

It is an offence to act as a charity trustee while disqualified, unless the Charity Commission gives a waiver under section 72(4) of the Charities Act 1993. So if this applies to you, either don't stand for appointment as a trustee in the first place or, if you are already a trustee, resign.

Practical requirements

It is equally important to look at the positive contribution you can make. You must be committed to the aims of the charity and able to give sufficient time to your role as trustee. This includes, as a minimum:

- attending trustee meetings and the annual general meeting;
- reading papers before each meeting;
- making a contribution during meetings;
- making decisions in the best interests of the charity;
- ensuring that the minutes of meetings accurately reflect discussions and decisions;
- making sure that you know enough about the charity to make informed decisions on its behalf.

However, trusteeship is much more than simple attendance at meetings. You have to ensure that paid staff and volunteers are properly managed and supported, and that the organisation is being efficiently run and is financially sound.

You may also be able to make a particular contribution to the charity.

- You may have certain key skills or knowledge (for instance, as an accountant or IT specialist) that is extremely valuable and could cost the charity a lot of money if it had to pay for it.

> ❝I started off years ago as treasurer of the toy library when my daughter was a toddler – I have a maths degree and no one else seemed to have much of a clue. And it's kind of gone on from there. My daughter's doing her A levels now, so I'm not doing the books for the After School Scheme any more, thank goodness, but I'm still treasurer of the allotment association and the local residents' association. I can't imagine not being involved in some sort of community group. ❞

- You may know some of the influential people in the area where the charity works; these contacts can be worth their weight in gold.
- You may have experience of doing the same kind of work as the charity (for example, if the charity is about adult education and you have been a teacher or volunteer tutor on an adult literacy scheme); if so, you can use these skills and experience on behalf of the charity.

> ❝It was because of my health research work that I was invited to become a trustee of a small healthcare charity. It isn't really all that time-consuming, and I feel that I'm doing something a bit more real, if you know what I mean. ❞

- You may be an enthusiastic fundraiser or event organiser, or good at involving and motivating volunteers.
- You may be a volunteer yourself, and so know what things are like at the 'coal face'.
- You may be someone who is or has been a beneficiary of the charity, and so can speak on behalf of other users and potential users of the charity's services – this is vital information for your fellow trustees.

> ❝The organisation is the best thing that ever happened to me. When I first came to see them, I was at the end of my tether, but they helped me to get back on my feet. I was pleased when they asked me if I'd like to be a volunteer – it meant that they believed I had something to contribute. I did that for six months and it seemed to go OK, but I was stunned when they said I should come along to a committee meeting to see if I'd like to join. They're all professional people and local councillors and so on. But they said that they'd really like to have someone who'd seen it from the other side, so to speak... ❞

This is by no means an exhaustive list. However, you and the charity will get much more out of your trusteeship if you feel that you can make a special contribution on top of your basic duties and responsibilities.

The best management committees have different people contributing different skills. In that sense it's an advantage if you don't have the same experience and contacts as your fellow trustees. A committee full of accountants should mean that you have excellent financial systems, but you may have only a very narrow perspective on the organisation's wider work. However, a committee with no legal or financial expertise may find itself fairly regularly grinding to a halt through lack of specialist information in key areas.

3 Why be a trustee?

There are many different reasons why people become trustees. First, charities need them! No trustees, no charity. Trustees move on, the charity's needs change, and even in an established charity it is good to have the new ideas, new energies, new perspectives that new trustees can bring.

You should also find it personally highly rewarding and stimulating. You are putting your skills and enthusiasms to good use in a new environment. You are doing this for free because you think the charity is doing something really worthwhile.

    " The most rewarding thing about being a trustee is watching young people develop, grow in confidence and fulfil their objectives. **"**

    " I got involved because I believe in promoting organic practices, and this seemed to be a good way to do it. **"**

Being a trustee also offers a terrific opportunity to help change things for the better. All charities are – or should be – looking to make a positive contribution to society, whether this means improving the environment, helping children find new ways of learning or expressing themselves, giving communities better facilities, changing people's attitudes to others, or generally improving the quality of life of individuals and communities. It is hard work; there are failures as well as successes. But as a trustee you should be able to look back with pride on the changes you have helped bring about, on the people who have grasped new opportunities – and your particular role in making this happen.

4 Why refuse to be a trustee?

No one is, or should be, forcing you to become a trustee. Just because a charity needs a trustee and thinks you fit the bill doesn't mean you have to say yes. If you don't agree with, or can't become particularly excited about, what the charity is doing, don't become a trustee. A useful guiding principle is to ask yourself whether you would become a member of this charity, raise money for it or become a volunteer (time permitting). If the answer to these questions is no, then you probably shouldn't become a trustee either. There may be nothing wrong with the charity; lots of other people – including your friends – may be diehard supporters and great evangelists for it. But if you don't rate it – with or without good reason – don't become involved.

You may feel you have nothing particular to offer. If this is just lack of confidence on your part, that should not stop you becoming a trustee. However, if all you can genuinely see yourself doing is turning up to meetings, saying little or nothing at them, and then voting with the majority, you will not be doing yourself or the charity any favours by becoming a trustee.

Equally, it may be the charity that doesn't really want you and your contribution. Some charities see trustees as a legal necessity and nothing more. Or the other trustees may think that they know best, that theirs is the only way, and expect you simply to fall in line. Either way, if that's the case you are not going to derive much satisfaction from your involvement, so find a charity where you and your contribution will be valued.

5 How long should you remain a trustee?

This is a difficult question. First, it will take you time to get up to speed as a trustee. You need to come to grips with what the organisation is doing, how it does it, its financial arrangements and how its particular group of trustees functions. It is also important to have continuity of trusteeship. If trustees keep coming and going, it will be much harder to generate a sense of purpose and organisational cohesion. Both these points are arguments for committing to being a trustee for a basic minimum of three years, but more likely for over five years.

However, there is also the opposite danger that the management committee never changes, or that it remains dominated by a few long-standing members. This can make generating or accepting new ideas much more difficult. New proposals may be met by remarks such as, 'For those of you who are new, we've never done it like that,' as if this were a clinching argument.

It is important to maintain a balance between experience and fresh ideas. Some charities set maximum terms of service. For example, the constitution may state that each trustee is elected for a period of three years, after which they must seek re-election. The charity may add a rule that no trustee can be re-elected more than twice (making a maximum of nine years) before having a break. There is nothing to stop such a person standing again after they have had a year or more out (although there is no guarantee of being re-elected).

There is no requirement to have a maximum 'length of service' rule of procedure. However, it is important to look at trusteeship from two angles:

- Are you still feeling motivated and committed, or are you burned out and rather disenchanted? If the latter, is it time to take a break?
- Is the organisation becoming too complacent, too set in its ways? Or does it actually need stability and continuity? It may be that you need to persuade people to stay, or that you should bring in new blood.

People become and remain trustees for all kinds of motives. They think it will help their standing in the community or their job prospects; they hope to make some useful business contacts; or they see themselves as a knight in shining armour coming to rescue some poor charity from the clutches of inadequate trustees. But ultimately trusteeship is about making a positive and willing contribution to something that you think is worthwhile. And that doesn't mean to say that you have to do it for ever.

PART **TWO**

Key roles of trustees

6 The role of the management committee

The management committee (or trustee group) is the governing body of a voluntary organisation. It is where the decisions are made and it is the body which is held to account for all the activities of the organisation. And it is the group responsible for ensuring that the organisation operates properly and effectively.

The role of the management committee can be summarised under eight headings.

Giving direction to the organisation

The management committee should ensure that the organisation has a clear sense of direction and purpose. If you don't know what you are doing, how can you function effectively? This vision must be shared by all the committee members, and communicated to the staff and others.

One way of communicating your vision is through a mission statement. This is a short, clear statement covering some or all of the following: why your organisation exists, what you do, how you do it, who you benefit and where you work.

Example of a mission statement

The Samaritans is a registered charity based in the UK and Republic of Ireland that provides confidential emotional support to any person who is suicidal or despairing; and that increases public awareness of issues around suicide or depression.

However, your vision is not much use unless you can put it into practice. This requires planning. Many organisations write up their ideas in a strategic plan in order to help review developments and monitor progress. This may be done by the chief executive/director, but should be discussed and agreed by the management committee.

For more detail on giving direction to the organisation see *Understanding your organisation* on pages 24–34.

Managing people

You are responsible for making the very best use of the people at your disposal. This includes both paid staff and volunteers. You need to ensure that the organisation:

- finds the people it needs to do the work (recruitment and selection);
- helps new people to settle in so that they understand the organisation, its values and what is expected of them (induction);
- allocates tasks for them to do;
- supervises and appraises what they do;
- supports and advises them where necessary;
- provides training where it is needed.

Many of these tasks may be delegated to a sub-committee or to staff. However, it remains the overall responsibility of the management committee to ensure that the people who carry out your work do so as effectively as possible.

For more detail on managing people see *Understanding your staff and volunteers* on pages 35–42.

Managing finances

Your financial responsibilities are absolutely key to your role as trustee. The trustees together are responsible for the financial health and good financial management of the organisation, for the money that comes in and goes out of the organisation. This includes ensuring that:

- bills and salaries are paid on time;
- money received is banked promptly;
- you have procedures for handling cash and signing cheques;
- any surplus money is invested to obtain a good return;
- you have annual budgets to show what money you expect to spend and receive;
- you monitor progress against these budgets and, where necessary, revise your plans in the light of developments;
- your annual accounts are produced on time and to the correct format;
- in general, you don't make financial commitments that you cannot meet.

Although the more detailed financial accounting and planning may be done by others (say the treasurer or finance officer), all trustees remain responsible for the financial performance of the organisation. Each trustee must develop a basic understanding of finance.

For more detail on managing finances see *Understanding your finances* on pages 43–49, and *Dealing with numbers* on pages 98–105.

Managing resources

Not only are you expected to manage the human resources (staff and volunteers) and financial resources (money) at your disposal, you are also responsible for ensuring that the other necessary resources are in place and in good order. This includes ensuring that:

- your property is kept in good order;
- your equipment is well maintained, correctly used and properly insured;
- there are sufficient funds for the organisation to carry out its activities – or, if not, that you have a workable fundraising plan.

For more detail on managing resources see *Getting the resources* on pages 50–59.

Managing yourselves

The management committee is responsible for managing itself. This includes:

- holding regular and effective meetings, where you share information and make decisions;
- members feeling committed to the organisation and working together for the good of the organisation as a whole – it is a team effort;
- having a full complement of management committee members, each understanding their role and making a positive contribution;
- ensuring that you each receive enough information to make good, informed decisions.

For more detail on managing yourselves see *Getting the work done* on pages 65–81.

The legal role

The committee must ensure that the organisation obeys the law – and there are quite a few laws to obey. For example: charity law, company law (for charitable companies), employment law, health and safety law, equal opportunities law, data protection rules, and regulations relating to premises, insurance and protecting the public. You will also need to keep track of legislation affecting the particular areas in which your organisation works.

This book is not principally about your legal responsibilities, although we touch on this in *What makes a good trustee?* on pages 1–15. There is a good deal of information available from other sources. The Charity Commission produces a series of free leaflets on various aspects of charity life, all written from a legal standpoint (see page 112 for more details). It also sends out a free twice-yearly newsletter to all registered charities, and has a telephone helpline. There is also a companion to this book, entitled *Charitable Status*, which gives you a basic overview of the law and your responsibilities.

However, a word of reassurance. You don't have to be a legal expert to be a charity trustee; you simply need to act sensibly. But don't be afraid to ask questions. If you feel you are out of your depth on a particular issue, seek advice from your fellow trustees, outside experts, the Charity Commission or whoever. As we said earlier, if you act prudently and in the best interests of the charity, you are unlikely to run into serious difficulties.

Accountability

A person or an organisation becomes accountable when powers or resources are delegated to them. They have to account for the way in which they use these powers or resources. Accountability is not a one-way process; it flows in different directions.

There are various people who will be accountable to you as they are carrying out tasks that you have delegated to them. These include:

- staff and volunteers;
- sub-committees;
- contractors (for example, builders and electricians upgrading your premises; outside trainers running training courses for your organisation; consultants helping you draw up a business plan).

As a committee member you are accountable to a number of people and organisations:

- donors and funders – you are spending their money in line with undertakings you made to them;
- regulators and rule-makers – those who check that the money is being spent properly and that the activity is allowed;
- beneficiaries or users of your services;
- members of the organisation;
- the wider community that benefits from your work.

Some forms of accountability (such as producing annual accounts) are compulsory; others are a matter of good practice.

For more detail on accountability see *Being accountable* on pages 60–64.

Maintaining independence

The independence of management committee members is absolutely crucial. No charity or trustee should be controlled or manipulated by others, or simply act as a representative of someone else's interests. Even where an outside body or person has the right to appoint or nominate a trustee, once the trustee is in place they must make decisions solely in the best interests of the charity, irrespective of the wishes of the nominating body.

Equally, the management committee should be careful to ensure that the organisation has a good spread of income and that it does not become overly dependent on any single funder. (For more on creating a fundraising strategy, see *Getting the resources* on pages 50–59.) Your main responsibility is to your beneficiaries; always try to maintain the freedom to act in their best interests.

And finally ...

Keeping your eye on these various balls, and taking necessary action, is the essence of good governance and being a good trustee. Always be prepared to ask the awkward – or even obvious – question, and make sure you find the necessary information to do your trustee job properly. That's what the rest of this book is about.

7 Understanding your organisation

As a trustee you have to get to grips with a number of different issues and make key decisions. If you have a good understanding of what your organisation is about, and where it fits into the wider picture, you will have a solid base to do this. There are various elements to consider.

Need

Your organisation was set up to respond to a need: for example to provide affordable housing in your area, or safe places for children to play or for abused women to live, or to encourage participation in music and the arts. It is very easy to become so preoccupied with the running of the charity that you lose sight of the reason why you are doing it.

66 We'd been running successful courses for women returners for years – CV writing, confidence building, that sort of thing. But it was only when we started really listening to the women who came to our job club that we realised how important it was to add basic computer skills to the range of courses on offer. So many women saw having to use a computer as the main stumbling block to getting a decent job and, whether they were right or not, it was affecting their confidence quite badly. 99

A prime trustee responsibility is to maintain enough information about the needs you are aiming to meet and how these are changing. Be particularly careful to listen regularly to the views of your users, beneficiaries and members – they will be a valuable source of ideas.

Vision and aims

The management committee should share a vision of what it would be like if your charity were to achieve everything you want to achieve. Although it may be a long way into the future before it can be realised, this vision should help to inspire and motivate the organisation.

One of the most important tasks of the management committee should be to translate its shared vision into a clear, understandable set of aims. These aims are what the charity intends to achieve in the long term. You need to make sure they are:

- in line with your charitable objects;
- clear and understood;
- shared by as many people as possible associated with the charity – the management committee, staff, volunteers, users and beneficiaries, and supporters;
- kept up to date.

The aims should answer the question: 'Why does our charity exist?' They provide you with coherence and identity, give a sense of purpose to everything that you do, and govern the tasks, priorities and targets that you set to achieve your vision. If you lose sight of your aims, your charity will sooner or later lose its way completely.

Mission statement

As we saw on page 19, many organisations summarise their aims in a short, clear statement of what the charity aims to do, for whom, where and how. It gives people a short, easily understood guide to what your organisation is about and provides a unifying focus for everyone involved.

Examples

'Shelter is a national organisation working to improve the lives of homeless and badly housed people. Shelter is the national organisation with local solutions.'

Sometimes mission statements may be a bit longer. For example, the Directory of Social Change (the publisher of this book) has a mission statement as follows:

'The Directory of Social Change is an independent voice for social change. We help voluntary and community organisations become more effective by identifying and acting on the current, emerging and future needs of the sector. We do this by providing practical, challenging and affordable information and training.'

The Ramblers' Association says:

'The Ramblers' Association exists to facilitate, for the benefit of everyone, the enjoyment and discovery on foot of Britain's countryside and to promote respect for the life of the countryside.

'We protect rights of way; campaign for freedom to roam over uncultivated open country; and defend the beauty of the countryside. We organise walking and campaigning events through the year in support of our charitable aims.'

It is better to have something that actually describes what you are about than something that is short and snappy just for the sake of it.

Some organisations reduce their mission statements still further to a strapline or slogan which they put on all publicity. For example:

'Access to learning for the whole community'
(The Bridge Project, which offers adult education opportunities in north Liverpool)

'Furnishing homes, furnishing lives'
(The Furniture Resource Centre, which provides low-cost furniture to people in need)

'Information and training for the voluntary sector'
(The Directory of Social Change)

'Making mobility matter'
(Guide Dogs for the Blind Association)

'Conserving wild places for nature and people'
(The John Muir Trust, which buys and manages wild land)

All these are very basic summaries of the aims and activities of wide-ranging and complex organisations, but they put the core message across quickly and easily.

Your mission statement (and strapline if you have one) should be simple and jargon-free. You are not looking for glitzy advertising slogans. Rather, you are trying to lodge the basic idea of what you're about in the minds of people connected with your charity.

If you are stuck on writing a mission statement, ask each member of the management committee to write down in not more than three sentences what they think the organisation is about and why. Gather these together and identify the common themes and ideas so that you can weave them into a single statement. Then give this to someone who does not know your organisation. Ask them if it gives them an idea of:

- why you exist
- what you do
- how you do it
- who you benefit
- where you work

Priorities

Your aims are likely to be fairly broad and long-term. You will not be able to achieve them right away; even if you did try to do everything all at once you would most likely end up doing most things badly and achieve little or nothing. So you need to set priorities.

Your priorities will focus the organisation on its key areas of activity. Some priorities are ongoing (such as setting and monitoring budgets each year), but they are no less important because of that. However, there will be particular issues, needs or areas of activity that you want or have to address in the reasonably near future.

Example

Hamletsville Village Hall is facing financial problems. The management committee realises that there are broadly two problems:

1 The retired members of the village community do not use the hall in the daytime, so it is often left empty once the parent and toddler group has finished at 11.30a.m.

2 Some of the long-standing evening activities are now poorly attended, so the groups struggle to raise enough membership subscriptions to pay an adequate hire fee for the hall.

Therefore, the management committee sets two financial priorities for the coming year:

1 To set up a new lunch club for older people (a recent community survey showed there was particular demand for this). This is initially planned to take place two days a week, but that could increase if the demand is there.

2 To disband (or at least move to a less prime time) the indoor bowls league and set up a computer club in its place. The parish council has been awarded some European money and has offered to help with most of the costs of the club for the first two years because it is concerned about growing unemployment in the village.

The village hall committee is also concerned that the Disability Discrimination Act will require it to become properly accessible. The main issue is that the current toilets are not suitable for wheelchair users, so the committee decides that the hall needs a proper disabled toilet.

Also, the caretaker will be retiring in the summer. Who will replace him?

Some of the priorities here are long-term and wide-ranging (such as the overall financing of the village hall); others are one-off processes (such as appointing a new caretaker). Addressing all of them, however, should help you fulfil the village hall's longer-term aims.

Tasks

It is important to think through your aims, mission statement and priorities, and to keep coming back to them. Unfortunately, none of this actually gets any work done! You need to put your ideas into practice and make sure that you are clearly working towards fulfilling your priorities. This involves being clear about who is doing what and how.

So, in the example of the village hall, who will tell the remaining five members of the bowls club that they can no longer use the main hall on a Tuesday evening? Who is going to run the lunch club? How will you get people to and from the club? Who will sort out the health and safety issues? And who is responsible for raising the money for the disabled toilet and overseeing its installation?

The management committee can delegate each of these tasks. Again, this is an example of the governance/management split (see page 5). The management committee can set up sub-committees, or delegate the detail to staff and volunteers (see *Getting the work done* on pages 65–81 for more information). However, the management committee must know what is planned for the year and make sure that things happen.

Targets

It is vital to focus on results. Your organisation will mainly be judged on what it achieves rather than on its intentions. You may set up a lunch club but only have eight members rather than the 40 you expected. In one sense you would have fulfilled one of your priorities; but you would still feel as if you have failed.

And if tasks are to be completed well and on time, it is a good idea to set targets for each one. Ideally, each target will be SMART:

Specific
Measurable
Achievable
Related to a priority or longer-term aim
Timed (that is, with a deadline date for completion)

Your target for the lunch club might therefore be to have 20 people attending two days a week after six months – but only if your research shows that there are enough older people in the neighbourhood to make 20 a reasonable target.

Again, the management committee may well delegate the responsibility for setting targets, but you will still want to monitor progress and, where necessary, make adjustments to timetables and target numbers.

By seeing that there are clear aims, priorities, tasks and associated targets the management committee has a framework against which to measure the organisation's progress, an effective way of checking that you are keeping within your constitution, and a ready source of information on which to base reports to funders and other outside bodies.

The
NEEDS
you were set up to meet define your
AIMS
as summarised in your
MISSION STATEMENT
which is then broken down into current
PRIORITIES
and
TASKS
which are given
TARGETS
against which you can measure your
SUCCESS

like success to persuade funders that you are a good organisation which will make excellent use of their precious money. One of the main questions funders now ask themselves when considering an application for money is not, 'Is this a good idea?', but rather, 'If we give them the money, will the organisation be able to deliver results?' Showing that you have a good track record of achievements is one of the best ways of building outsiders' confidence in your organisation.

As a management committee, make a list of your organisation's five major successes of the last three to five years. What was so significant about them and what did they enable you to do next? Why do they show that you are a good organisation?

If you are a new organisation, make sure that you document successes as soon as you have them, and build up and communicate a sense of achievement.

Keeping track of history

Management committee members also need to know the key points in the organisation's development. These can include:

- when the organisation was set up;
- when you received your first significant grant;
- when you employed your first member of staff or your fifth volunteer (or whatever was a critical number);
- when you were first able to open all day, or three days a week, or whatever;
- when you had your hundredth user;
- when you moved into your first (or current) premises;
- when you elected your patron;
- when you had your first celebrity visit.

This list is by no means exhaustive. The key thing is to decide what were the particular milestones for your organisation. These may include some, or all, or none of the items on the list above. As with your main successes, you are looking for a list of, say, between five and ten key developments which show how far you have come, and how good and reliable your organisation is.

Keeping track of others

There may be plenty of organisations operating in your local community or your field of work. Or yours may be the only one. You need to know where you fit, why you are different or unique, who else is doing similar things, who you work with, who you don't want to work with, and – in general – why you are the best at what you do. There are various reasons for doing this:

- To justify your existence – there are currently over 180,000 registered charities in England and Wales alone, plus a further 4,000 registering each year; in an increasingly competitive fundraising environment you will need to explain why you are the best people to be doing what you do.
- To build on your strengths – you can't do everything, so do what you do best (which, hopefully, nobody else is doing, or at least not as well as you).
- To minimise the threat of being overtaken by someone else.
- To be aware of new opportunities which you could exploit to do new things or strengthen the organisation.
- To be aware of potential partnerships or joint working arrangements which may open new doors and give you greater credibility.

Some organisations set up smaller development committees to think about these issues and then report back to the management committee. Whichever way you do it, it pays to be well informed about your organisation, its strengths and weaknesses, its successes and its background. It all helps you make good planning and strategic decisions.

Policies

Policies are the broad frameworks within which your charity operates. They define and describe how you do things. They can be a good way for the management committee to feel reassured that things are operating properly.

For example, an organisation working with young people should have a policy on vetting new leaders, the ratio of leaders to young people, minimum numbers of male and female leaders, and so on. Such policies provide stability, as everyone involved can refer back to them for guidance on how best to proceed.

Similarly, all voluntary organisations should have policies on their financial management (sometimes called financial procedures). See *Understanding your finances* on pages 43–49 for more information on this.

The management committee plays a vital role in making sure that the organisation has relevant policies. There is a danger, however, that policies grind the whole organisation down; that you think you have to have a policy for everything before anyone can do anything. The basic aim of policies is to help ensure that routine tasks (such as record keeping) are carried out consistently and that there are minimum standards for the organisation.

You must also revise policies in the light of current needs, circumstances and legislation. Just because something was relevant three years ago does not mean to say that it is now.

Producing a policy is often a question of formalising what currently happens, or what appears to be common sense. There are a number of areas which you should think through, and for some you may choose to have a written policy:

- statements of principles or values which underlie the work;
- employing staff and volunteers;
- equal opportunities;
- ethical or moral principles – such as who (if anyone) you will not take money from, work with or generally be associated with;
- managing your finances;
- dealing with conflicts and crises.

And finally ...

By now you may be feeling that you will never have time to assimilate all the necessary information. But don't despair! As a trustee you cannot be expected to know everything; you are simply expected to know enough to take sensible decisions. The rest of this book looks at different ways of organising information so that you can find what you need and can operate really effectively.

8 Understanding your staff and volunteers

People are usually the most important asset in any voluntary organisation. They are also often the most undervalued (or at least they may feel that way). Relations with your staff and volunteers are governed by a mixture of legal requirement and good practice. However, you should see your staff as your biggest resource rather than a potential legal minefield. And, just like any other asset, they should be managed and developed for the benefit of the organisation.

> After you have read this chapter, it's a good idea to complete
> Checklist 3, *Employment and volunteers*, on page 91.

Paid staff

The management committee becomes an employer as soon as you hire paid staff. You need to take this role seriously because:

- You are responsible for seeing that staff work effectively towards achieving the objects of the organisation. If they don't, you are not managing the organisation's resources effectively.
- Staff rely on you for their livelihoods.
- Your organisation (and possibly even you personally) may face serious penalties if you do not obey the laws covering employment.

There is no single, right way to manage staff. You should develop a system that suits your organisation and ensure that it is implemented either by your director and managers, if your organisation is of sufficient size to have these, or by the management committee if you supervise your own staff directly. There are three general areas of policy to consider: staff development, equal opportunities and pay policy.

Staff development

You need to invest in your staff, to nurture them by providing opportunities for learning and development. This will encourage:

- personal and professional development;
- improved performance;
- people to work better together;
- the organisation to change and adapt to different needs and circumstances.

Staff development is often tackled under the following headings:

- *Recruitment and selection* – making sure that you produce accurate and realistic job descriptions and person specifications so that you attract and choose staff with the right skills and qualities for the job.
- *Induction* – preparing staff properly for their work.
- *Supervision* – ensuring that all staff are adequately supervised and can learn from their work and what they do (see *Appraising staff performance* below).
- *Training and development* – encouraging staff to go on training courses which will help them develop; some organisations set aside a certain amount of money each year for training and development.

Equal opportunities

You need to ensure that staff are employed fairly and that nobody is unfairly discriminated against. This is a matter of law as well as good practice. You can do this by:

- advertising job vacancies openly and widely;
- adopting selection procedures which are fair and focus on the job to be done rather than the people you know and like;

> **❝**When we looked carefully at the job description, we realised that it wasn't essential for the job holder to be able to lift and carry heavy boxes, since we already had three members of staff who'd been trained in manual handling. What was crucial was the ability to use a computer, so we revised the person specification to reflect this.**❞**

- providing regular supervision and training opportunities to help develop appropriate new skills;
- considering flexible working practices (part-time options, job-shares, flexi-time);
- taking account of childcare needs;
- making sure that your premises are accessible to people with disabilities;

- monitoring the make-up of the staff – in terms of race, gender, ethnicity and disability, for example – and the opportunities that these staff are offered (for instance, who receives promotion and training).

Pay policy

Your salary bill is often your biggest single item of expenditure. You need to know how decisions about pay are made and consider:

- what pay agreements already exist;
- what you need to pay to attract good enough applicants;
- what you can afford to pay;
- what other people in the organisation are paid and how each job relates to the others;
- what similar jobs in other organisations are paid.

A staffing sub-committee?

Staffing matters can take up a lot of time. Some of the above, especially your approach to flexible working patterns, are a matter for discussion and debate rather than absolute requirements. And these debates can become quite heated. Some organisations therefore set up a staffing sub-committee made up of people who have relevant skills and experience. The committee is usually charged with:

- developing and reviewing employment policies;
- promoting and encouraging training and development opportunities;
- advising on problems and issues as they arise;
- keeping up to date with changes in employment law.

Whatever the particular role of the sub-committee, it must report back regularly and clearly to the management committee, which remains responsible for all staff and the decisions affecting them.

Appraising staff performance

Trustees should ensure that a system of appraisals of staff performance is in place. There is usually a formal appraisal once a year, which is carried out by the employee's manager, with regular (say quarterly) reviews of progress. The starting point for any appraisal should be the employee's job description, together with a set of specific targets which should have been drawn up and agreed at the beginning of the year. The appraisal can then consist of a discussion of:

- which targets were achieved over the last year, and why;
- which targets were not achieved over the last year, and why;
- what the employee and manager agree are the targets for the coming year;

- what help the employee will need to do this (such as training);
- how success will be measured.

The quarterly reviews assess progress towards achieving targets, revising these in the light of any changed circumstances and checking that enough support is being given.

Appraisals work best when:

- there is an atmosphere of trust and honesty;
- the person being supervised is involved in assessing their own performance;
- the process is linked to training and development, rather than pay.

Some organisations operate a '365 degree' appraisal system where the employee is encouraged to comment on how they are being managed. This can be a valuable opportunity for a manager to obtain feedback on their own performance.

The chief executive

Your senior staff member (chief executive, director, chief officer, or whatever they are called) is the key link between the staff and trustees. The relationship is potentially problematic because he or she:

- may well have more relevant professional expertise than some of the trustees;
- will often know more about the work of the organisation;
- and yet is your employee.

In order to avoid problems:

- Always bear in mind the distinction between governance and management (see page 5); respect the judgement of your senior staff member and give them the backing that they need in order to manage the organisation.
- Keep the lines of communication open, so that you know enough about what is going on in the organisation to do your job as trustee, without becoming bogged down in the detail.

It is difficult to supervise by committee, so the task of supervising the chief executive is often delegated to the chair of the trustees, who may need help and guidance in this role – through an outside mentor, for example. It is usually a good idea to establish a framework of regular meetings where the chair and senior staff member can update each other and discuss current issues. These meetings can be an opportunity both to monitor and to offer support.

Legal responsibilities

There is a massive amount of legislation affecting employees, their rights and responsibilities. There are separate acts on health and safety at work, sex and race discrimination, equal pay, disabled persons, and employment protection (and that is by no means all).

As an employer, it is good practice to issue all staff with a formal contract of employment. This will be similar to any contract that you have had yourself as an employee, setting out the responsibilities of the employer and the rights and responsibilities of each employee. There is a model contract of employment in *The Voluntary Sector Legal Handbook* published by the Directory of Social Change (the book's details are on page 115 – or your local Council for Voluntary Service may have a copy: see *Useful addresses*, pages 106–107). Or you could base your contract on something produced by an organisation similar to your own. If you have a staffing sub-committee, its members could draft a contract of employment which the management committee could then discuss and approve.

As well as this, it is wise to have a written procedure for discipline, dismissal and grievances, which does not form part of the contract but which is made available to all staff. Although you always hope you will never have to refer to it, it is much easier to be prepared in advance with policies and procedures, rather than to be faced with having to draft something under pressure when things start to go wrong.

The management committee is also responsible for ensuring that income tax and national insurance are paid to the Inland Revenue, and for doing this on time. There are severe penalties if you fail to do this. If you are not sure exactly what to do, seek professional advice.

You need to have employer's liability insurance too. Again, you will probably need to seek professional advice on the sort of cover that is available.

Communicating with staff

Much of this book deals with the kind of information that you as a management committee member should be receiving. However, information must flow both ways. You need to make sure that your decisions and the reasons behind them are communicated effectively to everyone in the organisation. Otherwise, you will become very remote from the day-to-day work and find it harder to make informed decisions.

It is also important to encourage staff and volunteers. Always try to:

- Give positive feedback – it's easy to assume that people know when they are doing a good job and say nothing. Everyone needs encouragement.
- Give constructive criticism – people can only improve their work if they know which specific elements need to be improved. But try to be supportive rather than destructive.

Volunteers

Volunteers are the life-blood of many voluntary organisations. In fact, the majority of charities in Britain have no paid staff at all, and even some of the very largest are heavily dependent on volunteers to deliver their services.

However, you need to think carefully about your approach to volunteers. Just because they give their time for free doesn't mean that you should accept any and everybody who walks through your door.

Volunteering is a two-way process. Volunteers give their time, energy and skills; in return they receive various non-cash rewards (such as personal satisfaction, skills development, the opportunity to make a difference). You need to make sure that volunteers have clear roles to play and are properly briefed and well looked after. They must also have the necessary skills to do a good job, be supervised effectively and generally bring credit to the organisation. To help you achieve this, you can use job descriptions and person specifications to recruit and manage volunteers as well as paid staff.

> **❝** It was so encouraging to see people make the transition from using our services to volunteering to support other parents in similar circumstances. Some of our best mentors have been drawn from among our beneficiaries. **❞**

It is good practice to develop a policy document or code of practice on volunteering. Volunteers are a vital and valuable resource for your organisation. They give you their time and energy to help you advance your aims, so it is only fair that you manage them properly and provide them with a rewarding and worthwhile experience.

> **❝** Now that I've retired, I've got too much time on my hands – and I do enjoy meeting people. I really look forward to my Monday morning stint at the job club. My role is just to welcome people

and make them feel at home while they're waiting to see an adviser. Everyone says how much better the atmosphere is since we started this system. I feel that I'm part of a team that's doing something useful – and since I've got my bus pass, I don't cost them much! **"**

Investing in your volunteers

Many of the issues covered in the section on paid staff above also apply to volunteers. You need to make sure that sufficient resources are allocated in the budget to recruit, select, train, supervise and organise your volunteers. Someone within the organisation should be responsible for ensuring that every volunteer is supervised and contacted regularly, that they have the chance to discuss and plan their work, and that they receive positive feedback. No volunteer should feel out of pocket as a result of their activities; each one should feel that their organisation really does believe in the unique contribution they make, recognise it and want it to grow and develop.

Keeping volunteers motivated

Try to make sure that your volunteers:
- feel appreciated;
- have a sense of belonging to the organisation;
- feel part of a team with their co-workers;
- are treated as working partners by paid staff;
- receive recognition for their work;
- are involved in some of the decisions which affect their work (such as setting objectives and solving problems);
- feel able to handle the tasks offered to them;
- are given a chance for advancement and personal growth;
- can see that their work makes a real difference.

Volunteers and the law

There is a lot of legislation affecting volunteers. If they are receiving welfare benefits, there are limits on what they can do and what they can receive in expenses. Equal opportunities legislation also covers volunteers, as do health and safety laws. If volunteers work with children you should have a code of practice which takes into account important legal issues such as the need for obtaining a Disclosure from the Criminal Records Bureau. Once again, many organisations have found it helpful to set up a sub-committee to oversee their policies and practices regarding volunteers, or to specifically include volunteers within the responsibilities of the staffing sub-committee. The National Centre for Volunteering has helpful information on all aspects of volunteering (see *Useful addresses*, page 107, for details).

After reading this chapter, turn to Checklist 4, *Involving volunteers*, on pages 92–93 to find out if your organisation is making the most appropriate use of volunteers.

And finally ...

In general, try to make a point of talking to staff and volunteers both to find out what they think and to prevent a 'them and us' attitude from setting in. Although there is almost always some distance between staff and trustees (and probably rightly so) you are all part of one organisation, dependent on each other to get things done. Each person has their own particular role, but the better the relationship between you all, the more effective everyone will be.

9 Understanding your finances

Trustees are not expected to be accountants; nor do they have to understand every last detail of the accounting process. However, they are responsible for the financial health and good financial management of the organisation, so it is vital that each trustee has a basic understanding of finance. *Dealing with numbers*, on pages 98–105, takes you through a set of figures.

Anyone who has managed their own household affairs will have a basic grasp of budgeting, record keeping and forward planning. You may also have had responsibility for financial management in the course of your own paid employment. It is likely that your organisation will have either a paid member of staff (book-keeper or finance officer/manager) or a volunteer treasurer, whose job this is. As an ordinary trustee your role is to make sure that:

- your organisation has a proper system of accounting;
- you receive sufficient and regular information to oversee the organisation's finances effectively;
- you understand the accounts and can interpret the financial information you receive;
- the person who inspects or audits your accounts is happy with the way in which records are kept and accounts are produced, and has given your latest accounts a clean bill of health.

Accounting systems

Your basic accounting system should tell you how you are doing financially. This includes:

- where your money comes from (income accounts);
- what you spend money on (expenditure accounts);
- whether your income is greater or less than your expenditure (surplus or deficit);
- what income and expenditure are planned for the future (budgets);
- what are your assets and liabilities (balance sheet) – assets are

positive items such as cash in the bank, investments and money owed to you; liabilities are negative items such as money that you owe;

- what return you are receiving from investments and money in bank accounts (investment policy; use of cash balances).

If you are joining an organisation that already exists (rather than setting one up from scratch), make sure you understand how the current accounting system works.

> Completing Checklist 5, *Finances*, on page 94 will help you to judge if your organisation's procedures are appropriate.

Information from the accounting system

Your accounting system is the basis for the financial information that the organisation needs for its own internal purposes (your management accounts – see *Budgeting and financial planning* below) and for external reporting (annual accounts).

Larger organisations will do their accounts on computer; smaller organisations may keep handwritten records. Whichever system you use, you need to make sure that it is accurate and backed up by evidence (invoices, receipts, lists of cheques paid in and so on).

Charities have to keep their accounts in a certain form. Most are governed by the Statement of Recommended Practice, known as the SORP, issued by the Charity Commission (updated in 2000). The precise form of your annual accounts depends on your income.

- Small charities, whose income and expenditure are under £10,000 a year, need a simple receipts (income) and payments (expenditure) account, together with a statement of assets and liabilities.
- Charities whose income or expenditure is over £10,000 but under £100,000 can prepare the same accounts as small charities above, but these need to be scrutinised by an independent examiner.
- Charities whose income or expenditure is over £100,000 but under £250,000 must prepare full accrual accounts and balance sheet, and have them scrutinised by an independent examiner.
- Charities whose income or expenditure is over £250,000 must prepare accrual accounts and balance sheet and have them audited.

These are minimum requirements. Charities can elect to have audited accounts even if their income is below £250,000, or prepare full accrual accounts if their income is under £100,000.

Charitable companies, of whatever size, should prepare a Statement of Financial Activities (SOFA) in accordance with the SORP, plus a balance sheet, and have them audited.

Unless you are the treasurer, you are not expected to know the details of all the above. *The Charity Treasurer's Handbook* provides more information for those who need it (see page 114 for details). However, you must read and understand your annual accounts and seek clarification where necessary. It is always useful to compare this year's accounts with last year's to see what has changed, and find out why.

You also need to look at whether you are making a surplus (profit) or a deficit (loss). You may have made a deficit for perfectly understandable short-term reasons. For example, last year you might have decided to spend some of your reserves on buying three computers and a photocopier. Although you are confident that they will more than pay for themselves in future savings, this may have meant that you made a loss for the financial year in question. Alternatively, your deficit may indicate more fundamental financial problems that require some hard thinking. Large deficits also present fundraising problems, because funders will be concerned that you are financially incompetent or are gradually going bust. You may therefore want to attach a note to your accounts clearly explaining the situation, why it arose and what you are doing about it.

Surpluses are generally good news – unless they are too large, in which case they can present fundraising problems as well, because it could appear as if you can't use all the resources you have. Again, you might want to explain in your accounts if, for example, you have just received a large grant at the end of the financial year which will be spent over the following year.

Budgeting and financial planning

Your annual budget is your financial plan for the year ahead and a key management tool. It helps you to control expenditure and gives you advance notice of the income you need to raise. Make sure that the budgeting process is started early enough (at least three months before the start of the next financial year) to give you time to make critical decisions about staff recruitment or the level of your charges to users, for example. Although it is usually left to the treasurer (or paid staff) to draw up the budget, all trustees must be involved the process. You need to:

• Check that the budget reflects the plans and priorities of the organisation. Are you focusing resources on the work that is most important?

- Check the reasoning behind the figures. Will income actually rise as predicted? Why are costs increasing in any particular area?

The budget is then broken down into monthly or quarterly estimates of income and expenditure, because not all money comes in or goes out evenly over the year. You might have weekly income and expenditure from your lunch club, but the income from your annual garden party might all come in during July while the expenditure is mainly incurred in August, with a deposit cheque for the venue and marquees due in the previous November. Try to predict under each budget heading in which month money will come in and go out. You will then have a useful monitoring tool (see *Management accounts* below).

There is a tendency within the budgeting process to overestimate income and underestimate costs in order to make things look good. In practice, income tends to be lower than anticipated and costs higher. Make sure that you stress these points in your discussions, until you are satisfied that your budget is a reasonable and realistic document. This year's figures will often be a guide to what you can expect, unless you are predicting a significant change in your activities.

You also need to budget for reserves.

Reserves

Although as charity trustees you are under a legal obligation to use charity funds within a reasonable time of receiving them, you also need to plan carefully for the future. You need to have funds to protect the organisation in case you run into cash flow problems, or a regular grant is suddenly cut, or you experience a general downturn in income. Alternatively, there may be a new piece of legislation that means you have an unexpected jump in costs (to conform to new health and safety regulations, for instance), or your rent may be doubled after a rent review, or you may need to make some staff redundant.

More positively, it is always useful to have money that you can spend on the development of the organisation. For example, you may decide to buy in outside help to look at some key policy areas, to invest in IT, to produce new information booklets, or to undertake a major marketing and publicity operation.

All of this means that each charity should aim for a level of reserves which helps it to guard against problems and make the most of opportunities. Reserves are simply extra money in the bank (or invested elsewhere) that you can spend on any part of the charity's work or development. A reasonable level of reserves is now seen as a sign of good management, of taking sensible precautions in an increasingly volatile charity world.

Most organisations now aim to have at least the equivalent of three months' income as reserves. So, for example, if your annual income is £60,000, you would have at least £15,000 in the bank at the end of the year, after all bills are paid. Some organisations aim for a much higher level than this – as much as one year's income. You need to decide what level of reserves is appropriate to your organisation, plan how you aim to reach your desired level, and budget accordingly. You may need to do this over a number of years.

Cash flow

Cash flow refers to the flow of money in and out of the organisation, and when you expect these transfers to happen. If your experience up to now has been as an employee of a large company, you may never have had to worry about this. In a small charity where you have limited cash in the bank, cash flow can become a real issue. For example, although you may be budgeting for a surplus on the year as a whole, your main grant may not come in until after you have had to pay some big bills. So will you have enough money to cover these bills? Or what if a grant is paid later than you were anticipating? Will this mean your account goes overdrawn?

> **❝** I was so embarrassed. I'd completely forgotten that we'd have to pay everyone's travel expenses on the spot, even though we weren't paying for room hire or the tutor till the end of the month. We had to find over £100 in petty cash just when our bank balance was at rock bottom! **❞**

Your cash flow forecast is a monthly estimate of when money is due to come in, when it will be paid out and how much will be left in the bank. It should enable you to track progress and ensure that you can pay salaries, bills and expenses on time. If the organisation's account is expected to go overdrawn, you can then make arrangements in advance.

Management accounts

Management accounts compare the actual income and expenditure of the organisation with the budgeted figures. Sadly, writing things down in a budget, however carefully, does not guarantee that they will turn out as planned.

Management accounts are usually produced monthly in larger organisations and quarterly in smaller ones. Each income and expenditure budget heading is compared with the actual figure (taken from your accounting system) for the year up to that point. Trustees should then:

- note any significant differences between the budget and actual figures (for income and expenditure);
- try to understand why these have occurred;
- discuss whether you need to take any action – the discrepancy may be a one-off blip or it may be part of a longer-term trend;
- discuss whether you need to revise the budget in the light of this.

You need to strike a balance between not panicking at the first sign of trouble and not leaving things too late in the hope that problems will solve themselves. In general, try to keep a lid on costs. It is much easier to control expenditure than it is to raise extra income. Discussing your financial position should be an agenda item at every trustees' meeting.

Dealing with numbers, on pages 98–105, gives much more detail on reading management accounts.

Basic procedures

It is also worth checking that the basic accounting procedures are being followed through. For example, it is vital that:

- all money and assets are used solely to pursue the objects of the organisation as set out in its constitution;
- full, accurate accounting records are kept securely for at least seven years;
- bank accounts are operated properly and cheques are signed by more than one person;
- cheques are not signed without details of the amount of the payment and the purpose for which it will be spent;
- all payments are backed up by a source document (such as an invoice or a bill);
- petty cash payments are backed up with receipts;
- all grant money is spent in accordance with the terms on which it was awarded;
- the monthly payroll is checked and authorised by a senior staff member or trustee (and certainly not left to just one person to do);
- all necessary tax and national insurance are deducted before making payments to staff or for casual labour.

This may all be familiar to you from other contexts, but you may not be aware that if you are a registered charity you should also include the words 'registered charity' and your charity number on headed notepaper, cheques, invoices, orders, publications, publicity material and other official documents.

Finance sub-committee

Finance is one of those areas particularly suited to a sub-committee. The finance sub-committee is charged with regular scrutiny of the management accounts and any issues arising from them. The treasurer (or chair of the sub-committee if you don't have a treasurer) then reports to the full trustees' meeting. However, remember that even when the detailed scrutiny of figures is delegated, you and all the other trustees remain legally responsible for your organisation's finances.

And finally ...

In general, if you feel uncomfortable around figures or you cannot understand the information you receive, ask for help from your fellow trustees or a suitable person outside the organisation. Don't be embarrassed; it may simply be that the information is being produced badly, or is unnecessarily complicated. There is plenty of training around to help you understand accounts. Whatever you do, don't assume that you can simply leave it all to the others; they may be just as bewildered as you are.

10 Getting the resources

The management committee is responsible for making sure that the organisation has enough money to stay solvent, and to maintain and develop its work for the benefit of its current and future users. This usually requires some fundraising, whether this involves a series of coffee mornings or major applications to grant-making trusts. Once again, the trustees remain responsible for all the fundraising activities of the charity, although they may do very little fundraising themselves.

Trustees are also under an obligation to preserve and make best use of the assets and resources at their disposal, including ensuring that money is not left lying around in non-interest-bearing bank accounts.

This chapter starts with fundraising and then moves on to managing your assets.

Fundraising

Your fundraising activities and tactics can say a lot about your organisation. It is usually through your fundraising that most people come into contact with you, so you need to get it right. Your donors will be concerned about both how you raise your money in general and what you will do with their donation in particular. So, as a trustee you need to ensure that:

- fundraising is undertaken properly;
- the purpose of any appeal is clear and accurate;
- you do not use methods which exert undue pressure on people to give;
- you obey the law;
- money raised is properly accounted for.

You should be clear from the outset about how much money you need to raise, your strategy for doing this, and where the organisation will find the necessary resources (time, expertise, people, materials, administration) to achieve success. You can then monitor progress towards your target at regular intervals and keep a watchful eye on your fundraising costs.

Ethics

You should also have a policy on who you will and will not take money from. For example, the National Lottery Distribution Boards (which channel money, among other things, to charity, the arts, sport and heritage – see pages 109–111) all derive their money from gambling. Or perhaps a local company which has just offered you a £5,000 grant for your children's play area has suddenly laid off 300 people. Does this matter? Does it matter where your funders invest their money? And would you accept money from your local authority if in return it required a place on your management committee or a right to see your management committee papers and minutes?

The main rules on these kinds of ethical decisions are:

- It is not what you as an individual trustee thinks that counts. Your personal likes and dislikes are irrelevant. It's the best interests of the charity that matter. For example, you may be a trustee of an environmental organisation and you don't approve of nuclear energy. This doesn't necessarily mean that the charity shouldn't apply to BNFL, say, for money. However, if the trustees know that taking money from the company would risk alienating your supporters then it would be perfectly reasonable not to apply. The National Childbirth Trust (NCT), which among other things promotes breast-feeding, caused a bit of a storm among its members over whether or not it should accept money from Sainsbury's plc. The objection was that Sainsbury's markets its own brand of formula milk and that this goes against what the NCT believes. On another occasion, Nottingham University caused upset among its staff and students by accepting a major gift from British American Tobacco.

- If you want to reject a gift (certainly a major gift) on ethical grounds, you should first contact the Charity Commission for its approval.

Basically, there is no right or wrong on ethics other than what is appropriate for your charity, its members and its users. However, it is better to decide beforehand what you will and won't do and plan accordingly.

Six key fundraising concepts

1   Fundraising is about personal relationships. Somebody asks somebody for money. The better these two people know, like and trust each other, the more likely the potential donor will be to give. A lot of fundraising, especially at the local level, boils down to who

you know. If you don't know enough of the right kind of people yourselves, you might want to recruit into the organisation people who do, and get them to use these contacts to raise money (see *Organising your fundraising* below).

2 Fundraising is about change, rather than money. Donors give to help improve people's quality of life, or to protect the environment, or to support the arts, or whatever. Therefore, your fundraising approach should be to explain how you change things for the better rather than simply stating what work you do.

3 Fundraising tends to be about individual pieces of work (sometimes called projects) rather than the organisation as a whole. For example, an overseas aid charity will place an advert featuring a starving child in a newspaper and say, effectively, 'Help us work with people like this.' This is a much more powerful fundraising proposition than simply saying, 'Please give whatever you can to Save the Children.' Or a hospital will have an appeal for a new scanner rather than ask for a general contribution to hospital funds. Similarly, you may well need to break up your organisation's work into individual chunks and raise money for each one.

Examples of projects

- An alcohol recovery organisation raising money for an alcohol awareness programme in schools
- A community centre raising money for a new roof or a disabled toilet
- An arts organisation raising money for an exhibition of paintings by local children
- A conservation organisation appealing to save an area of outstanding natural beauty or a fine building
- A mental health organisation raising money for an awareness programme to combat prejudice about mental health

4 Fundraising must be relevant. Just because people or institutions have money doesn't mean that they will be interested in you. Make sure that you or your fundraisers have a good reason for contacting each person you write to or ask for a donation. If there isn't one, don't bother; concentrate your energies on more fruitful sources instead.

5   Most of your money may well come from a few key supporters or a few key activities (such as a regular fundraising event). It's very easy to take these for granted and put all your fundraising energies into pursuing new sources of income. This is a recipe for disaster. People who have given before are the most likely to give again, as long as you have looked after them. The book *Looking after your Donors* covers this in detail (see page 114 for information).

6   You can't tell funders everything – there isn't time and they won't listen to (or read) it all. So tell them about what is most likely to interest them.

Sources of income

The general public are still by far the biggest givers to charity (currently giving about £5 billion a year, £1 billion of which is left in wills). They give through collections, fundraising events, sponsored events, radio and television appeals, direct mail requests, lotteries, because they are members of the charity, or simply because a friend asked them. There is no limit to the ways in which you can persuade people to give, and some of the oldest forms of fundraising (especially sponsored events) remain some of the best. There are plenty of books available which will tell you more.

Grant-making trusts are charitable bodies that exist to donate money to other charities. Each has its own interests, priorities and procedures. There may well be local trusts in your area, and there are also trusts that give throughout the UK (including well-known foundations like the BBC Children in Need Appeal). Collectively they give over £1 billion a year. There are directories which list trusts and what they will fund (see *Publications* on pages 112–115). You may need to decide whether to invest in copies of these or to consult them through your local CVS (see pages 106–107) or public library.

The National Lottery was set up to generate funds for charity. It currently channels over £1 billion a year to charities, the arts, sports and heritage projects. There are different distribution boards, each with its own interests and, unfortunately, fairly complex applications procedure. However, there is also an excellent small grants scheme (Awards for All) for organisations with an annual income of less than £15,000. More information is available through the phone numbers and websites listed under *National Lottery Distribution Boards* on pages 109–111.

Companies give around £500 million a year to charities. Most receive far more appeals than they can handle, but many are from people they don't know. One of the best ways of raising money from a company is through their employees (for instance, persuading an employee who knows you and your work to raise money for you and to ask their company to match their fundraising), or through personal contacts with the company chair or managing director. Again, directories are available which give contact details for companies that make donations.

Government gives around £2 billion a year to charities, either in the form of grants or – more commonly – contracts for agreed work. Much of this comes through local authorities and health authorities and often consists of payments for basic services (such as meals on wheels, or childcare and health advice work). There are also major government funding programmes. The best way to find out about these is via the internet (see *Government funding* on page 111).

More and more charities are now earning income from selling goods and services. Some charge for the services they offer; some sell goods made by the beneficiaries of the charity; some sell t-shirts, Christmas cards and donated goods. You should note that trading through shops or catalogues usually doesn't make anything like the profits people assume, so enter into it carefully.

Planning your fundraising

Fundraising, like anything else, needs planning. Your organisation's strategic plan will highlight the main developments that are anticipated over the next one to three years. Each of these can be costed and fundraising targets set. Your annual budget shows what income is needed to keep your current activities going over the next year.

In addition to costing your work, you will also need to consider your fundraising costs. The biggest item of expenditure is likely to be the salary of a paid fundraiser or fundraisers – if your organisation has reached this stage in its development. Even if it hasn't, you will still be faced with decisions: do you make do with two-year-old copies of directories or invest in a brand new CD-ROM to help with your fundraising? Do you need improved internet access or a laptop computer? What about your public image? Is this the year to spend money on a logo and professionally designed leaflets? If all of this is going to be too expensive, are there other ways of obtaining the resources that you need? What does your local CVS have to offer? Can you obtain sponsorship from a local company?

Much of your fundraising may be regular and ongoing. The further you move away from this core support, the more expensive and time-consuming it becomes. So, try to think strategically about your current fundraising:

- Who are your supporters now?
- Why do they support you? What are their interests and concerns? Is any of this likely to change?
- How can you strengthen the relationship you have with your current supporters?

It may be that by simply retaining the loyalty and commitment of your current supporters you can continue to raise all the money you need.

The next stage is to look at potential new supporters (see *Sources of income* above):

- Which people or funding bodies do you plan to attract as supporters in future?
- What are their interests and concerns? And crucially, why should they be interested in your work?
- Realistically, what are your chances of raising money from them?

All donors have particular interests and concerns; the fundraising challenge is to show that you address these concerns.

Organising your fundraising

The management committee should think through who will do the work of asking for money. This will depend on who is willing, who has the skills and time, and whether you have or can take on staff to do it.

If you employ fundraising staff you can expect them to do most of the fundraising leg-work. However, trustees often still play a very active part here, particularly in making direct approaches to individuals, trusts and companies and, in general, making maximum use of their personal contacts.

You may decide to delegate the fundraising to a committee. The members of a fundraising committee do not all have to be trustees, although like any other committee it should report back to the trustees regularly. The committee's main responsibilities are drawing up the fundraising plan and making sure it is put into practice. This may involve:

- delegating some of the fundraising tasks (such as writing grant applications) to existing staff;
- bringing people with good contacts on to the committee – they can help ask for money;

- employing and managing a fundraiser (subject to budgetary approval by the trustees);
- setting up other sub-committees to undertake particular aspects of fundraising (such as organising events or obtaining legacies);
- setting up an appeal committee to organise and oversee a large fundraising appeal.

The fundraising committee should be made up of people who are committed to raising the money, who enjoy doing it and have the appropriate skills. But overall responsibility for ensuring its success still lies with the management committee.

Getting the max

There are various tax incentives to encourage people to give which you should try to take advantage of. Charities can reclaim the tax on any donation made by any taxpayer as long as:

- the donor provides a Gift Aid declaration (which replaces the old Gift Aid certificate), and
- the charity maintains an 'audit trail' linking the payment to the donor – in other words, as long as the charity records each donation separately so that it can prove to the Inland Revenue how much each donor has given.

The Gift Aid declaration can state that it covers all donations from the date of the current gift onwards, so one declaration covers all future claims. There is, however, a limit on the level of benefits the donor can receive (broadly, 2.5% of the value of total donations, up to a limit of £250).

So, in theory, you can add 28% (on 2000/01 tax rates) to the income from a sponsored run if:

- all your sponsors are taxpayers;
- they all sign or have signed a Gift Aid declaration;
- you can prove that they have made the payment.

Donors can also give you shares rather than cash. This may become a really popular way of giving among the more affluent.

Three words of caution

1   There are various laws covering fundraising. They mainly concentrate on avoiding theft and misleading the public. There are also specific regulations on lotteries, raffles and tombolas, public collections and using external fundraising consultants. For further information, see the books listed on pages 113–114.

2   In fundraising it is very easy to become funder-led: doing what you think you can raise money for, rather than what you and your users want. Chasing money because it's there may work in the short term; however, after a while the organisation will start to fall apart as people drift away, saying, 'This is not what I got involved for.'

3   Try to strike a balance between scattering your fundraising energies over too many sources, and being over-dependent on a single source. You have to have an awful lot of resources if you are to keep a large number of fundraising pots warm; on the other hand, reliance on a single funder can put you right in their pocket.

In general, in your fundraising try to build on your current strengths and successes. If you have a successful annual event, what can you do to make it even better? If you have a key funder, what are you doing to maintain and develop your relationship with them so that it bears fruit for many years to come? Or are you just assuming – or hoping – that this will continue to go well?

- Fundraising is simple, but not easy. It is not rocket science; don't be seduced by fancy jargon. However, it is often a lot of hard work and you need to make sure the work is done.
- Fundraising is friend-raising. Relationships are the key. The more personal your fundraising, the more effective it will be.

Managing your assets

The other side of getting resources is making the most of what you already have. Your organisation's assets fall under five headings: equipment, property, stock, cash and investments.

Equipment

You must make sure that all your organisation's equipment is properly recorded. This asset register should list all your equipment, giving details of date of purchase, supplier, purchase price, warranties and maintenance agreement.

Equipment should be properly serviced, maintained and insured. People using it should be properly trained, and health and safety regulations enforced.

Property

Any property that you own or rent must be kept in good condition and insured. Also, if you are letting out space make sure that you are receiving the best possible returns.

Stock

If you keep stocks of goods for sale, such as publications or merchandise, make sure that:

- there is a system for keeping records of stock;
- all stock is safely and securely stored;
- it is fully insured;
- the quantity is in line with what you expect to sell, and is not too out of date;
- you keep an accurate record of stock values.

Cash

You should be receiving maximum interest on the cash you hold. You need to:

- know where cash is held, in what sort of accounts (current, bank deposit, building society), the interest you earn and the charges you pay;
- have a system to move cash balances to interest-bearing accounts as quickly as possible;
- make sure you have access to money placed in high-yielding accounts when you are likely to need it.

Investments

If you have large cash balances, look at the high-interest options, including the money markets. The Charities Aid Foundation has a money deposit scheme (CAFcash) specifically for charities (see *Useful addresses*, page 108).

However, unlike a commercial company a charity is limited in its investment powers. Your constitution may further limit what you can do. In any case you must be very careful to spread the risk across a range of investments, and regularly review your investment performance so as to minimise risk and maximise returns.

And finally ...

Once again, trustees need to keep a balance between time and responsibilities, between governance and management. If you become too heavily involved in fundraising activities (and this is easily done) you won't have enough time for the important strategic and policy decisions. However, there's no point in having a marvellous business plan and no cash to finance it. By spreading the load, and through appropriate delegation, the management committee should be able to ensure that all bases are covered. Just because there is a lot to do, especially on the fundraising side, it doesn't mean that you as an individual trustee have to try to do it all.

11 Being accountable

A person or organisation becomes accountable when powers or resources are delegated to them. They have to account for the way in which they use them. Accountability flows in different directions. If you delegate to someone else they become accountable to you. But as a charity trustee you are held to account for the conduct and activities of your organisation.

Unless there is a real need for confidentiality, you should always be ready to explain and justify the policies you have chosen to adopt. Charities are expected to be open in their dealings, with their donors, with their members, staff and volunteers, with the public and with the Charity Commission.

Different types of accountability

Donors give money to a charity to undertake certain work or to achieve certain things. The trustees are accountable to the donors for how the money is spent.

In a membership organisation, the management committee has power delegated to it by the membership to govern the association in accordance with the constitution. The committee is accountable to its membership.

All charitable organisations are expected to work for the general public good. In return, they receive tax and other advantages. Charities are delegated power by the general public to work on their behalf. They are therefore accountable to the public, which includes the requirement to send their full accounts to anyone who asks for them in writing.

Registered charities must account for their activities to the Charity Commission. This includes sending their annual report and accounts to the Commission, plus completing an annual return (for further information on the different accounting requirements for different organisations, see *Understanding your finances* on pages 43–49).

The annual report

One of the key ways of accounting for your actions to all your different constituencies is through your annual report. Many people regard producing the annual report as a chore, but it can be a vital marketing and publicity tool. Too few organisations make full use of their annual report, so it is worth giving it serious thought. (For more details, consult *How to Produce Inspiring Annual Reports* – see page 114 for information.)

If you are a charity, there are certain legal aspects to your annual report. It should account for:

- your financial affairs;
- your progress in pursuing your aims;
- your effectiveness in achieving your objects;
- the key people involved (management committee and senior staff).

However, the fact that the report needs to contain certain information doesn't mean it has to be dull. A good annual report will:

- Include a brief statement of your overall aims and mission.
- Contain brief, enthusiastic reports on the work your organisation has done and its achievements during the year. (As with fundraising letters – see below – you won't be able to say everything, so say what is most interesting and relevant to your readers.)
- Include relevant facts and figures, case studies or descriptions which capture the quality of your activities or services.
- Assess progress over the year, highlighting achievements and reflecting on key challenges.
- Contain photographs and diagrams, not just words.
- Use short paragraphs and sub-headings to break up long portions of text.
- Use pie charts or summaries of financial information, rather than a full set of accounts.
- Be lively and readable so that it will be noticed and read.

Although the management committee is ultimately responsible for the report, you are unlikely to achieve the best results if you try to write it as a committee. Delegate responsibility to one person, who should have a clear timetable and procedure allowing for comments and contributions from trustees at the appropriate point.

Other ways of reporting

The annual report alone may not be enough to ensure that everyone is kept informed. You may also need to:

- produce simple leaflets or brochures for wider circulation;
- get on local radio and in newspapers;

> **❝** I never realised how easy it is to get on local radio until I did my first press release for the project. The local weekly paper reproduced it word-for-word at the bottom of a column somewhere, but the local radio station called me in to do a live interview. It seemed to me that they were quite desperate for content. **❞**

- hold open meetings with members, users and beneficiaries;
- produce formal reports according to set criteria for official funders such as a local authority or one of the National Lottery Distribution Boards;
- report in person to key people (such as major donors).

In general, you should be looking to see that the organisation is promoted effectively, and that this is done in keeping with its aims and values.

Reporting to funders

Many funders make it a condition of their grant that they receive both your annual report and accounts, plus a more detailed report on how you have spent their money. They like these reports to concentrate on outputs and achievements. In jargon terms they like to know about:

- *Inputs* – what goes into the organisation, the resources and effort the organisation spends on its different activities.
- *Processes* – the way in which the work is done.
- *Outputs* – the specific achievements, numbers of people benefiting, targets met.
- *Outcomes* – the impact of the work done in meeting a need, solving a problem, creating change.

Inputs and *processes* relate to what the people in your organisation do and the way they do it. *Outputs* relate to what the organisation does for its users and beneficiaries. *Outcomes* show what impact you have made on the needs you set out to tackle. You should concentrate on your achievements in terms of outputs and outcomes, and especially on evidence from your users and beneficiaries that they are happy with what you do and how you do it.

Accountability to users

Your users or beneficiaries are key voices in your planning, monitoring and reporting of processes. It is not enough simply to decide what you think your users might want and then go full steam ahead. Your funders, members and supporters will all want to know that the people you exist to help are happy with what you are doing. There are various ways of receiving feedback:

- using surveys and questionnaires;
- conducting interviews;
- setting up monitoring groups where trustees, staff and users discuss progress;
- having users on the management committee.

It is always worth having positive quotes or testimonies from users in publicity material.

Staff and volunteers

There is a two-way accountability process between staff and trustees. First, the staff and volunteers are responsible to the management committee, which has delegated certain tasks to them but which remains responsible for all the activities of the organisation. There are a number of ways of monitoring this:

- Receiving reports at management committee meetings – it is usual for the chief executive to present a report on progress and events since the last meeting; you may wish to receive additional reports from individual departments or on particular activities.
- Setting up steering or sub-committees to oversee particular aspects of the organisation's work and development.
- Talking to staff, volunteers and service users.
- Visiting projects or activities to see the work at first hand.

A measure of tact is needed to ensure that staff and volunteers feel you are genuinely interested in their work and take your responsibilities seriously, but that you are not trying to do their job for them. The boundaries between governance and management can often become very blurred in small organisations.

It is equally important that staff and volunteers feel part of things, that their ideas and actions count and are valued. You should make sure that management committee decisions are communicated to the staff – as well as, where possible, the reasons behind them. You also need to ensure that staff have proper supervision and support and that they feel the management committee is pulling its weight (see *Understanding your staff and volunteers* on pages 35–42).

Members and supporters

If you are a membership organisation, you will have to account to your members formally at your annual general meeting and informally through newsletters and other publicity materials.

Annual general meetings are sometimes seen as unfortunate legal necessities, or as opportunities for people to meddle unnecessarily in the affairs of the charity. However, it is much better to use them as opportunities to celebrate the year that you have had, look forward to the opportunities and challenges ahead and, in general, galvanise, enthuse and re-motivate the organisation. It is important that the chair's report sets a positive and constructive tone, and that all members of the management committee are on hand to meet and hear from the organisation's members and supporters.

Newsletters are good ways of keeping in touch with members. As with your annual report (see above), keep them lively and upbeat, maybe inviting views and contributions from members, supporters, staff, volunteers and key contacts. They don't need to be glossily produced, although they should appear consistent with the values and status of your organisation. Make sure that you keep an eye on all the costs involved, from design, print and production through to time spent on putting them together and sending them out: newsletters can become a problematic drain on organisational resources as well as a terrific asset.

And finally ...

In general, you should aim to be as open as possible in your dealings with people and monitoring organisations. Obviously, you will have confidential information that it would be inappropriate to discuss; and there may be discussions going on (say over strategy) that for the time being are best kept private. That is a matter for your judgement. But as a rule it is better to involve people rather than exclude them.

PART **THREE**

Getting the work done

12 Organising your meetings

As a trustee you have a number of responsibilities and a lot of work to get through. Management committees must meet together to make decisions, share information and ensure that the organisation is being effectively managed. However, you do not have unlimited time, so committee members need to work effectively together to complete the tasks required in the allotted time.

The management committee is responsible for running itself. One of the most important aspects of this is ensuring that you hold effective meetings. There are various ways of doing this, and you need to choose the method which best suits you. However, you should bear the following points in mind:

- The committee as a whole is responsible for making meetings effective. It is a team effort.
- The chair has an important role in meetings, but is one among many, and relies on the positive contribution of all members.
- The agenda is the main tool for organising the meeting. Like all tools it can be used well, or abused.
- A relaxed climate in which all trustees feel able to participate is essential.
- Members must observe proper standards of confidentiality.
- Members must feel committed to, and work co-operatively for, the organisation as a whole.

Working through Checklist 6, *Committee meetings and decision making* (see page 95), will provide you with some more useful pointers on this topic.

Why hold meetings?

Your constitution will require the management committee to hold a certain number of meetings a year. However, meetings are not just about fulfilling your legal responsibilities. You also hold meetings to:

- decide the strategy and policies for the organisation;
- agree objectives, priorities and plans;
- receive information to monitor progress;
- solve problems;
- make decisions on what needs to be done and who should do it;
- ratify decisions made elsewhere (for example, by sub-committees);
- share views and opinions;
- educate committee members about the work of the organisation and the issues that affect it;
- provide support and social contact between committee members.

You can't do all of the above all of the time, so committee members need to be aware of the purpose of each part of the meeting.

You should guard against allowing the management committee to become bogged down in administrative detail. For example, there may be an agenda item to decide on the purchase of a computer. The committee should be clear about why there is a need for a computer (this may be to hold membership details, to do the accounts, or whatever) and take a decision accordingly. However, it should not try to choose which computer to buy. Leave that to a member of staff or delegate it to an individual trustee. Keep the committee's eye on the bigger picture.

When do you hold meetings?

As we have already said, your constitution will require you to hold a minimum number of meetings a year. However, in most organisations you will need to meet more frequently than this. It is up to each organisation to decide how often is appropriate. As a general rule, if you are meeting fewer than four times a year the management committee will become sidelined and powerless; if you are meeting more than once a month the management committee is doing too much and should delegate more.

Some organisations adopt a system of regular meetings of the whole committee (say six times a year), and interim meetings of one or more sub-committees to keep an eye on particular areas of operation.

The agenda

The main tool for organising your meetings is the agenda, as this sets out the plan for the meeting. It is much more than just a list of headings. Each agenda item should tell management committee members exactly what will be discussed and why, so that they can prepare properly for the meeting.

There are five main reasons why an item may be on the agenda for the meeting:

* to report – to give information, ideas or opinions to the meeting;
* to consult – to obtain information, ideas or opinions from people at the meeting;
* to discuss – to talk about an issue or problem, but without coming to a conclusion or decision at that meeting;
* to resolve a problem – to hear as much as possible about a particular problem and come to a conclusion about how to deal with such difficulties, but without necessarily deciding to take specific action now;
* to make a decision – to decide to take action about something.

You need to be clear about each item on the agenda. Ask yourself (and, if necessary, others):

* Why is this item on the agenda? What result do we want to achieve by considering it?
* If the item is not appropriate for discussion at the management committee, where should it be dealt with?
* Who will be responsible for any action agreed?

Good meetings need good, clear agendas rather than vague lists of discussion topics. It is also important that members stick to the items on the agenda. Otherwise, you will wander all around the houses, achieve nothing, and end up with everyone frustrated and disillusioned.

Effective committee meetings

The management committee operates through meetings. The best meetings are where people can work together in an atmosphere of trust and commitment to achieve agreed results. An effective committee has:

* the right kind of members, with appropriate skills, experience and knowledge;
* a clear and agreed purpose;
* a good size (generally between 5 and 15 members);
* an effective chair;
* a positive atmosphere;

> **❝**I actually enjoy committee meetings. I get a real sense of like-minded people pulling together over something they believe in.**❞**

- good administration (agendas and relevant papers);
- good record keeping (minutes);
- confidence that decisions will be implemented.

Plan social time before or after the meeting. This means that people have the chance to chat in an informal environment and get to know each other better, but without this intruding on the meeting itself. You may not go so far as to have a fully timed agenda, but always have a start and a finish time, and don't go for more than 90 minutes without a break.

You may want to set some explicit ground rules, such as:
- It's OK to ask questions.
- If in doubt, ask.
- Keep contributions brief and to the point.
- Don't just repeat other people's contributions.
- Listen to other people's contributions.
- Don't interrupt.
- Don't use jargon and abbreviations unless they are explained.

You will need someone to act as secretary. This can be the same person each time or the task may be done in rotation. Whoever takes the minutes should take care to note all action points, with a name or names next to each one. They should try to summarise the main points of discussion, but there is no need to attempt a verbatim record of everything that was said. (See also *The secretary* on pages 74–75.)

Ineffective committee meetings

It's fairly easy to derail committee meetings through inappropriate behaviour. Try to guard against the following:

Intimidation – some people are so sure of their own views and position that they have no time for anyone else's. Alternatively, people may be so attached to their ideas and arguments that they take questions or disagreement as personal criticism.

Rushing – it's important to talk things through. What seems a perfectly good and straightforward idea to one person may not be particularly clear or acceptable to another. Also, ideas may have wide-ranging financial implications. Even though it would be really good to adopt a particular course of action doesn't mean that you automatically go ahead and do it: you may not be able to afford it.

Agenda dyslexia – jumping about, or even off, the agenda. Stick to the matter at hand, even if a discussion about last night's television or about world poverty would be more interesting.

Proceduralism – using knowledge of committee rules, however obscure, to thwart decisions.

Nit-picking – raising obscure points of detail to undermine confidence, even after the decision has been made. You don't have to sort out every last detail before the committee can decide to go ahead.

Negativity – try not to focus just on the reasons why something might not work, or require yet more information before you make a decision. There will be many occasions when you say, effectively, 'On balance, this seems like a good way ahead.' There may be forceful arguments against, but better ones for doing it.

Recklessness – just 'giving it a go', or saying yes because you want to leave on time. Decisions need to be thought through and discussed properly.

As with most things in management committee life, you need to strike a balance between undue caution and reckless optimism; between giving space for and valuing everyone's contribution, and allowing the discussion to go round and round in circles; between procrastination and railroading. The chair needs to be particularly vigilant, keeping the meeting positive and moving things forward at an appropriate speed.

Making decisions

Most constitutions require decisions to be made by simple majority voting. In practice, most decisions are made by general agreement rather than a formal vote. This is fine when there is a general consensus, but can lead to problems when there is not.

> **❝** Committees work best when everyone takes responsibility – rather than leaving everything to the chair – and everyone plays a role. This helps create a positive atmosphere for debate. **❞**

The chair should make sure that:

- members are always clear what decision they are being asked to take;
- any views for and against the decision have been heard;
- there is clear agreement on the decision – if not, move to a vote;

- voting is minuted, so that anyone who disagrees can ask for their disagreement to be recorded;
- there is a summing up at the end of each item, noting the decision and action required.

It may be that you cannot reach a decision yet, because you need more information. However, don't use this simply as an excuse to avoid making hard choices.

In general, you have to steer a course between efficiency and decision making on the one hand, and sensitivity and inclusiveness on the other. If one or two dominant committee members simply railroad decisions through meetings, the remaining trustees will become disillusioned and drift away – or at best only make a minimal contribution. Equally, decisions have to be taken, even when not everyone agrees.

Staff attendance at committee meetings

The paid employees of a charity are not generally allowed, by law, to be voting members of its management committee. However, staff can take part in discussions and their attendance can help relationships and communication between committee and staff. The management committee can always ask for staff members to leave the meeting if they want to discuss matters privately.

In smaller organisations, with not more than two or three staff, it can be helpful for all members of staff to attend management committee meetings to speed up the information flow and build a sense of joint working. In larger organisations, this is impossible.

The most senior staff member usually attends meetings. Other staff members can either attend regularly because of their role (for instance, the finance manager may need to provide information to the treasurer and committee), or attend by invitation to discuss matters of particular relevance to their work. Large organisations often involve the whole of their senior management team in management committee meetings.

And finally ...

Much of your trusteeship will revolve around meetings, especially management committee meetings. Try to make sure, as far as possible, that the meetings are well structured so that you can make a valuable contribution while listening to the views of others, and that the decisions you make reflect the combined wisdom, experience and expertise of the whole committee.

13 Special roles on the management committee

Although all trustees are responsible for everything that goes on, there are three key bases to cover, namely those of chair, secretary and treasurer. Even if you don't use all these titles (not every voluntary organisation has a treasurer, for example), you need to ensure that the functions are well covered.

The chair

The chair has to ensure that the management committee functions properly, that everyone is able to contribute fully during the meetings, that all the items on the agenda are discussed and that effective decisions are made. The position of chair is difficult but key. The chair is expected to provide leadership, but must not dominate the meeting or inhibit the contributions of other members. They must also know the rules for the conduct of meetings, as set down in the governing instrument.

And it is not simply a question of chairing meetings. The role of the chair includes:

- Being a figurehead of the organisation. This will often include representing the organisation at other meetings, speaking on its behalf and attending public functions.
- Making sure that the management committee operates effectively, that it is made up of suitable, active and committed members with the appropriate mix of skills and experience to run the organisation.
- Ensuring appropriate supervision of staff. The chair often directly supervises the senior member of staff in the organisation.
- Assisting with the management of the organisation. The chair may find her/himself involved in some of the managerial tasks of the organisation. This could involve overseeing budgets and expenditure, signing cheques, liaising with the treasurer, signing letters and participating in the recruitment of new staff.

Acting as a chair can be a time-consuming business. It is important that the person chosen has the time as well as the skills to bring to the role.

" Our chair is a lecturer at the university. Although she seems to put in incredibly long hours, her timetable is pretty flexible, so she's generally available for meetings, even at short notice. And the political skills she's developed in academic meetings are just what's needed to keep our rather eccentric bunch of trustees in order! **"**

The secretary

Most constitutions require that there is a secretary to the trustees. In organisations with paid staff, secretarial duties can be delegated to a staff member. Where there are no paid staff, the secretary is an important and time-consuming role for a trustee or volunteer.

A key task is minute taking. The minutes are a legal record of the decisions taken by the management committee. They are checked by all committee members and, once approved, are signed at the next meeting by the chair. The decisions are legally binding.

Minutes should give a clear, accurate record of decisions taken. They are not full transcripts of the meeting. Rather, they:

- summarise the key points made in discussion;
- record decisions taken;
- identify what actions were agreed, who is responsible for doing the work and by when.

Each set of minutes should also include the date of the meeting, a full list of who was present and when the meeting started and finished. When summarising discussions, don't include names or personal references unless there is a particular reason for doing so – for example, when a trustee wants to record opposition to a decision. (For more information see *The Minute Taker's Handbook* – details on page 115.)

Some organisations ask a non-trustee to be minutes secretary, as this then frees all trustees to take a full part in the meeting. If this is the case, the secretary will not have all the responsibilities listed below, so the chair may have to take on some or all of these instead.

Other tasks of the secretary include:

- keeping a check on the progress of the work agreed by the management committee;
- ensuring that the organisation meets its legal obligations, including reporting to the Charity Commission and meeting charity law requirements;

- checking that there is a quorum at meetings (your constitution will require a minimum number of members to be in attendance before a meeting is legally valid – this minimum number is called a quorum);
- making arrangements for the meetings (booking the room, arranging refreshments and so on);
- preparing the agenda (with the chair);
- circulating the agenda with papers and previous minutes well in advance of the meeting;
- checking that members have followed through agreed action since the last meeting;
- keeping a list of trustees, plus addresses and telephone numbers;
- ensuring that members are informed of annual general meetings and any special meetings;
- maintaining records of correspondence.

The job of secretary can be demanding, especially for someone who is not very well organised. It can be one of those jobs that you only really notice when things go wrong; but where it is well done, it can relieve the chair of a considerable administrative burden.

> 66 I've been a PA for 20 years. I had a really solid, traditional secretarial training – including shorthand! I'm not very good at speaking in public, and I felt I wasn't contributing much to meetings, so I was relieved when they asked me to be secretary. 99

The treasurer

The treasurer's job is to monitor the organisation's finances on behalf of the whole board, to report regularly on them to the board, and to make sure that money and property are properly managed. The treasurer does not necessarily do all the book-keeping, record-keeping, budgeting and such like, but needs to make sure that they are done and done properly. This requires:

- proper systems for budgeting, financial control and reporting to be in place;
- procedures to reduce the risk of fraud;
- all trustees to be kept properly informed about the state of the organisation's finances;
- financial reports to the trustees that are comprehensible and properly discussed;
- accounts and other financial reports to be produced in the proper

form and on time as required by other bodies (such as the Charity Commission);

- competent auditors or an independent examiner to be appointed, according to legal requirements.

But even if you have a treasurer, remember that all trustees are responsible for the organisation's finances and for getting sufficient financial information about the organisation.

14 Delegation

Ultimate responsibility for running a voluntary organisation rests with the management committee as a whole. However, there can be a lot of work to get through, and you may want to spread the load by having others take on different bits of the workload.

66 It is vital to have a sense of shared responsibility, of having common goals, instead of a 'them and us' attitude. We need to recognise that people have diverse skills and make sure that we use these skills creatively in the team. 99

You can delegate tasks to individual committee members (such as appointing a treasurer to oversee the finances), to sub-committees, working groups, managers, staff, volunteers or specialist advisers. However, always remember:

- Although you can delegate the task, you cannot delegate legal responsibility – everything that the charity does ultimately comes down to you, even if you are not aware of what is being done.
- Delegation can lead to confusion about who is supposed to be doing what – you need to provide a clear brief so that people know what is expected of them.

Sub-committees

The management committee of a small organisation can usually carry out most of the business itself, and does not need to delegate work to sub-committees. However, as the organisation becomes more complex it may be helpful to set up small committees with delegated powers to carry out a particular role.

Typical sub-committees include:

- finance committee – to oversee the financial affairs of the organisation;
- finance and general purposes committee – to oversee financial, general staffing and management matters; this committee often meets between management committee meetings to keep an eye on things generally;

- fundraising committee – to oversee the fundraising strategy and organise fundraising events;
- staff committee – to oversee staff management and development;
- project committee – to oversee the work of a particular project or development.

A key feature of sub-committees is that they are set up to be ongoing and are part of the formal structure of the organisation (shorter-term committees tend to be called working groups – see below). The chair of each sub-committee is usually a trustee and therefore sits on the main management committee. This helps to ensure clear lines of communication (see below).

The main advantages of sub-committees are that they:
- are focused on a small range of tasks;
- can recruit members with particular expertise or experience;
- can involve staff members in areas relevant to their work.

The main disadvantages tend to be:
- communication between them and the management committee can break down;
- they can be seen as powerful cliques – the place where the real decisions are made before being rubber-stamped by the management committee;
- they require even more time from management committee members;
- their roles may not be clearly defined and can overlap with the remit of other committees, causing confusion and duplication;
- they may want more independence and freedom of action than the management committee is prepared to give them;
- they may cease to have a valid purpose, but continue to meet in any case;
- individual committee members see it as 'their' committee and are difficult to remove.

Each sub-committee must therefore always have its own, very clear brief (see below).

Working groups

A working group is less formal than a sub-committee. It is set up to deal with a particular task or issue. It has a limited life-span and is dissolved when it has completed its work.

Many of the advantages and disadvantages of working groups are the same as those for sub-committees. One difference is that working groups tend to include a much higher proportion of staff and volunteers; this means they can become a forum either for positive debate and engagement, or for moaning and complaint.

Working groups are often set up to look at issues such as:

- equal opportunities or anti-racism policies;
- feasibility studies (for example, moving to new premises);
- specific problem areas (such as staff development opportunities);
- organisational structures;
- the implications of new legislation.

For example, an equal opportunities working group may be asked to:

- review the organisation's equal opportunities policy in the light of current legislation and best practice;
- assess significant areas of weakness or under-representation among management committee, staff, volunteers and service users;
- assess how the organisation promotes and publicises itself and its activities from an equal opportunities perspective.

Having done this, the group may be asked to draft:

- a revised statement of intent on equal opportunities, outlining the organisation's commitment to equal opportunities;
- a revised code of practice, outlining how the organisation will implement equal opportunities in relation to the recruitment and selection of management committee members, staff and volunteers; conditions of employment and volunteering; the recruitment of members and users; the provision and publicising of services and activities.

Alongside this, it could also be asked to:

- highlight and prioritise key decisions and actions that need to be taken;
- propose ways of monitoring progress in these crucial areas.

Working groups generally have fewer decision-making powers than sub-committees do; their role is more advisory. However, it is important to spell this out in advance, to avoid frustration and disappointment later.

Providing a clear brief

Much confusion can arise in the delegation process if it is not clear exactly what is being delegated. Job descriptions have a vital role to play in clarifying what is being entrusted to a particular individual. In the case of a committee, is it just being asked to provide information to help management committee members make a decision? Or is it supposed to be putting forward proposals or recommendations to the management committee, or even taking the decision itself? It can be tricky reining in a committee once it has exceeded its powers; it can be even more difficult overturning a decision that has been unilaterally taken and announced by a sub-committee when the management committee was expecting to discuss the matter itself.

Therefore, whenever a committee is set up it should have a clear brief (often called terms of reference). This brief should spell out:

- the purpose of the committee or working group – what it is aiming to achieve and what results are wanted;
- the powers of action (plus the limits to these powers) and the decision-making delegated to the committee – whether decisions need to be ratified by the management committee;
- how long the group is there for – whether it is permanent or has a limited life-span;
- how and when it should report back to the management committee;
- who should be on the committee, and why;
- how they should be appointed;
- how often the committee should meet;
- the role of the chair and minute-taker in meetings;
- who receives copies of the minutes;
- who convenes the meetings.

People need to know exactly what they are expected to do when they join a sub-committee or working group. Only then can they decide whether they have the time, interest and expertise to make a worthwhile contribution. If they don't, there is no point in them being there.

Maintaining communication

Good communication between the management committee and the sub-committee – or person with the delegated authority – is vital. With sub-committees or working groups this is usually a question of reading minutes and/or receiving reports at management committee meetings. The appointment of the chair of the committee is also key, both in terms of the communication process and to keep the committee focused on the task(s) in hand.

There are various ways in which staff should report to the management committee about tasks delegated to them. A committee meeting should always include a chief executive's report, summarising the main events and developments since the last meeting. The committee may also request other staff members to report on particular projects or areas of activity. However, much of the rest of the reporting will be more indirect, through appraisals and supervision sessions conducted by staff (see *Understanding your staff and volunteers* on pages 35–42).

And finally ...

In general, you need to think about how you spread the management load. The management committee may well not be able to do everything. Also, joining an over-burdened and frustrated management committee is hardly an attractive prospect for a potential newcomer. So think about breaking down the organisation's activities into manageable tasks which can be delegated, and then work out the most appropriate structure for doing this. However, always remember to keep control – because the management committee is the one which will have to answer for everything that is done in the name of the organisation.

PART **FOUR**

Getting the most out of being a trustee

15 Pulling it all together

You are under no formal obligation to enjoy being a trustee. You can be as miserable as you like (and some are!). However, you should find that trusteeship is rewarding. Although there are certain things the committee can do to make sure its members are satisfied, such as giving proper back-up and support, the following is a basic guide to getting the most from your trusteeship.

> Checklist 7, *Personal effectiveness*, on page 96 provides a summary of the points you should work through if you want to make the most of your role as trustee.

Know what is expected of you

Make sure you understand what being on the management committee involves, both in principle (understanding your responsibilities and liabilities) and in practice (forming a realistic picture of what the charity expects from you). You don't want to end up agreeing to do something, only to find that you haven't either the time or the skills to play the role expected of you.

Don't worry unnecessarily about your liabilities

Take your role seriously, but don't spend your whole time worrying about your liabilities if things go wrong. Take a balanced view, and evaluate any risks carefully. But don't let the organisation grind down through a constant fear that something may go wrong. If you've evaluated the risk and on balance it seems a good move, then do it.

Get to know the other trustees

Try to build up a good working knowledge of the skills and experience that the other members of the committee bring to the work. Try to build trust and rapport with your fellow trustees, although because trustees meet fairly infrequently this can take a lot of time. Social time before or after the meeting can be really helpful.

Keep informed about the work of the organisation

Keep in touch with what is going on. If possible, visit the organisation reasonably regularly and chat with staff, volunteers and beneficiaries. This should help keep you in touch with the needs that the organisation is trying to meet, and with the values and spirit within the organisation. You should also derive a lot of satisfaction from seeing the work being done well and appreciated; this is what you as a management committee member are trying to promote.

If in doubt, ask

You need to be well informed. If you are unclear about anything, ask. No question is too obvious or too basic.

Know where to go for information and advice

There will be a good deal of knowledge inside the organisation and on the management committee. You will have professional advisers too (lawyers, accountants and so on). There are also agencies, such as local Councils for Voluntary Service, which exist to help and advise local voluntary organisations (see *Useful addresses* on pages 106–107).

Don't become overloaded with details

Your main job is to keep a clear overview of the affairs of the organisation, its strategy and development. Don't become bogged down in day-to-day details. Delegate these to sub-committees, working groups and staff. Remember the distinction between governance and management.

Take an interest in a particular area

Try to develop an interest in an area of the organisation's activities. Give time to a sub-committee or working group, or develop an area of specialist knowledge. You might even do some volunteer work for the organisation in addition to your trusteeship. This will not only bring you into contact with fellow trustees and staff members, it will also help you feel that you are making a special contribution.

Be prepared

Make sure that you allocate enough time to read minutes and committee papers before meetings, and make a note of areas where you want more information or that you are particularly concerned about.

Follow things through

If you agree to do something, make sure you do it and within an agreed timescale. There is nothing more frustrating for management committees than when its members agree courses of action which are then simply not followed through.

Set priorities for your work

You know what your interests and skills are. Give priority to the areas which make best use of them. Avoid the temptation to say 'yes' to everything. You have limited time, so make sure that you and the organisation get the best from it.

Go to meetings

This may seem a statement of the obvious. However, it is the central point of your commitment, and it is massively de-motivating for your fellow trustees if they feel that they are the only ones making an effort to attend meetings. In any case, you are responsible for all the decisions taken at the meeting whether or not you were in attendance.

Review your work as a committee member

Ask yourself periodically whether you are still enjoying your trusteeship, whether you are being used most effectively, or even whether it is time to move on.

Reclaim out-of-pocket expenses

You give your valuable time free to the organisation. You should not be expected to bear the out-of-pocket costs you incur. The management committee should make sure that it has clear, simple and quick systems for repaying the out-of-pocket expenses of committee members.

Pat yourself on the back occasionally

You have decided to give your time voluntarily to something you believe in. Make sure that you recognise and value the contribution that you are offering, because you are helping the organisation do something really worthwhile in the lives of its beneficiaries or the community.

And finally …

Your work as a trustee matters. It makes a real difference. Enjoy it!

Checklists

This section contains a series of checklists. They pick up some of the core themes of this book and are designed to help you improve the effectiveness of both your management committee as a whole and your personal contribution to it. You may find that there appear to be lots, or even too many, areas for improvement. If so, don't be too downhearted about it. This is not a test or an exam. And in any case, all committees have room for improvement. Choose the areas you think are most important and start work on those. Then come back to the checklists in a few months' time and see where you've got to. If you're happy with the areas you have been working on, choose some new ones. Enjoy the process!

Checklist 1   The legal and management framework

1   Is it absolutely clear who is a full voting member of the management committee, and who does not have voting rights?
Yes ☐   No ☐

2   Do all members of the management committee know what our legal structure is?
Yes ☐   No ☐

3   Do all members of the management committee know whether we have charitable status?
Yes ☐   No ☐

4   Do new members of the management committee receive an induction pack containing background information about the organisation, its constitution (or summary), its main activities and areas of operation, finances, funding, current key challenges, plus the minutes of the last two management committee meetings?
Yes ☐   No ☐

5   If we have sub-committees, is it clear what decisions they can make?
Yes ☐   No ☐

6   Do we have a library of basic voluntary sector management books available to management committee, sub-committee members and staff?
Yes ☐   No ☐

7   Do management committee members each take a special interest in one or more areas of the organisation's activities or management issues, and act as a resource person for the organisation on that issue (for example, contracts of employment, health and safety, equal opportunities, fundraising, charity law, insurances, IT, PR, aspects of the organisation's services)?
Yes ☐   No ☐

Highlight the items ticked 'no' and assess what further action needs to be taken.

Checklist 2 Governance

1 Do management committee members know what we are
permitted to do under our charity's objects?
Yes ☐   No ☐

2 Do management committee members spend time occasionally
discussing the ethos or values which underpin our work?
Yes ☐   No ☐

3 Are management committee members aware of how our activities,
services and campaigns further our objects and reflect our values?
Yes ☐   No ☐

4 Do we regularly consult with our members, service users, staff,
volunteers and others interested in our organisation about how we
could develop?
Yes ☐   No ☐

5 Do we have a strategic plan?
Yes ☐   No ☐

6 Does the management committee receive regular financial reports,
plus reports on the wider progress, activities, problems and plans
of the organisation?
Yes ☐   No ☐

6 Do we have a process for defining our aims and priorities for the
next 12–18 months?
Yes ☐   No ☐

*Highlight the items ticked 'no' and assess what further action needs to
be taken.*

Checklist 3   Employment and volunteers

1   Are management committee members aware how many people we employ, what kind of contracts they have and how different posts are financed?
Yes ☐   No ☐

2   Do our employees receive written terms and conditions within two months of starting work, and do these comply with current employment legislation?
Yes ☐   No ☐

3   Do all employees have a written job description, and is it reviewed at least once a year?
Yes ☐   No ☐

4   Do we have a clear policy for paying volunteer expenses?
Yes ☐   No ☐

5   Do all employees and volunteers have an induction programme?
Yes ☐   No ☐

6   Do employees and volunteers have access to training?
Yes ☐   No ☐

7   Do we have a clear management structure so all employees and volunteers know who they are accountable to, and who they should go to if they need information or support?
Yes ☐   No ☐

8   Do all employees and volunteers have a regular opportunity to discuss their work progress and problems with a manager, management committee member or other appropriate person?
Yes ☐   No ☐

9   Does the senior staff member meet regularly with a management committee member to discuss progress and problems, and to review the senior staff member's work?
Yes ☐   No ☐

10   Do we have clear disciplinary and grievance procedures?
Yes ☐   No ☐

Highlight the items ticked 'no' and assess what further action needs to be taken.

Checklist 4 Involving volunteers

1 Have we considered why we want to involve volunteers, what they bring to our work that is special or different, and whether they are the best way of getting the work done?
Yes ☐   No ☐

2 Does each volunteer have a clear job to do – one that is appropriate and offers real job satisfaction?
Yes ☐   No ☐

3 Do we have an equal opportunities policy for volunteers, and a system of monitoring it?
Yes ☐   No ☐

4 Do we have a system of recruitment and selection?
Yes ☐   No ☐

5 Do we take up references (especially where the volunteer will be working with children)?
Yes ☐   No ☐

6 Are volunteers given job descriptions, informed of working conditions, properly briefed before they start, and told who they report to and how?
Yes ☐   No ☐

7 Do volunteers have regular meetings with a supervisor to discuss progress, problems and achievements?
Yes ☐   No ☐

8 Do we provide training and development opportunities for volunteers?
Yes ☐   No ☐

9 Do we provide out-of-pocket expenses for volunteers?
Yes ☐   No ☐

10 Do we provide information about our organisation to keep volunteers informed?
Yes ☐   No ☐

11 Do we provide information on how volunteering affects welfare benefits (where appropriate)?
Yes ☐   No ☐

12 Is the volunteer's voice heard in our organisation's planning
processes?

Yes ☐   No ☐

13 Do we have clear policies on the relationship between volunteers
and staff?

Yes ☐   No ☐

14 Can volunteers take on greater responsibility or change jobs within
our organisation?

Yes ☐   No ☐

15 Do we review the way our organisation involves both volunteers
and paid staff?

Yes ☐   No ☐

*Highlight the items ticked 'no' and assess what further action needs to
be taken.*

Checklist 5 Finances

1 Do the finance sub-committee (if there is one) and management committee receive regular financial reports, setting out income and expenditure for the year to date, comparing these with budgeted income and expenditure, and giving an explanation of major differences between actual and budget figures?
Yes ☐   No ☐

2 Does the treasurer understand that s/he is responsible for monitoring our finances on behalf of the management committee, and must report regularly to us?
Yes ☐   No ☐

3 Does our treasurer have a level of financial awareness and skill appropriate to our organisation?
Yes ☐   No ☐

4 Is the management committee aware of whether the organisation's accounts must be audited or examined by an independent person?
Yes ☐   No ☐

5 Do we have procedures to reduce any risk of fraud?
Yes ☐   No ☐

6 Do we have procedures to ensure that money is kept as securely as possible (e.g. keeping the absolute minimum cash on the premises, and keeping it in a securely locked place)?
Yes ☐   No ☐

7 If the organisation owns furniture, equipment, vehicles or other assets, does it keep a list of these assets, when they were purchased and their purchase value?
Yes ☐   No ☐

8 Does the management committee receive a report each year setting out the insurances that the organisation has (and does not have), with recommendations for changes?
Yes ☐   No ☐

Highlight the items ticked 'no' and assess what further action needs to be taken.

Checklist 6 Committee meetings and decision making

1 Do we receive good, clear agendas for meetings, setting out items to be covered and whether they are for information, discussion or decision?

Yes ☐   No ☐

2 Do we receive good background papers to the agenda items before meetings, clearly setting out the key issues?

Yes ☐   No ☐

3 Are agenda items properly introduced so everyone knows where we are up to, which are the relevant papers and what are the main issues?

Yes ☐   No ☐

4 Does the chair keep the discussion focused on the agenda item, ensure that everyone who wants to speak has the opportunity to do so, summarise fairly, and help the group to reach decisions?

Yes ☐   No ☐

5 Do all participants in the meetings act responsibly, keep to the point, value everyone's contribution and not become too heated or personal?

Yes ☐   No ☐

6 Do the minutes of meetings accurately reflect the decisions made, action required to implement these decisions, and the main points leading up to the decisions?

Yes ☐   No ☐

Highlight the items ticked 'no' and assess what further action needs to be taken.

Checklist 7 Personal effectiveness

1 When I receive papers for committee meetings, do I always read them carefully before meetings?
Yes ☐   No ☐

2 Do I make a note on the papers of any questions or points I want to raise?
Yes ☐   No ☐

3 If I want to raise matters which are not on the agenda, do I notify the chair before the meeting?
Yes ☐   No ☐

4 Do I make every effort to get to meetings on time?
Yes ☐   No ☐

5 If I know I am going to be absent or late do I notify the chair, secretary or other appropriate person?
Yes ☐   No ☐

6 If I arrive early, do I make a point of talking to new people or people I don't know very well?
Yes ☐   No ☐

7 During discussions, do I listen to what people are saying, rather than half-listening while working out my own response, making comments to neighbours, or thinking about getting home?
Yes ☐   No ☐

8 Do I genuinely respect and value other people's views?
Yes ☐   No ☐

9 If I disagree with a point do I present my views calmly and clearly, without being manipulative, aggressive or intimidating?
Yes ☐   No ☐

10 If we are discussing a matter in which I or someone else close to me has, or might have, a financial interest, or from which we might benefit, do I always declare this conflict of interest?
Yes ☐   No ☐

11 Do I volunteer to undertake tasks for the management committee or sub-committees?
Yes ☐   No ☐

12 If I do volunteer, am I clear what I have committed myself to?
Yes ☐   No ☐

13 If I take on something I can't do, do I notify an appropriate person in good time so that alternative arrangements can be made?
Yes ☐   No ☐

14 Do I keep confidential all sensitive information I receive as a management committee or sub-committee member, especially information about personnel matters and service users?
Yes ☐   No ☐

15 Do I do my best to keep up-to-date on matters relevant to the organisation's management, services, campaigns and other work?
Yes ☐   No ☐

Highlight the items ticked 'no' and assess what further action needs to be taken.

Dealing with numbers

Some people really like finance, enjoy working with figures, are really confident about what numbers mean. However, for the rest of us ... !

This section tries to help you through the numbers maze. It looks at a set of management accounts and explains what the numbers mean and how you work out what they might be saying. The accounts are based on a mythical community centre, somewhat unimaginatively called Anytown Community Centre. Further information about the centre is given below.

There is also outline information on the difference between management accounts and annual accounts.

Before you read the rest of this section, it may be worth re-reading *Understanding your finances* on pages 43–9, as it lays out the basic ground covered here.

About Anytown Community Centre

This is a community building which runs a range of activities from within the centre as follows:
- a playgroup (paid for partly by a grant from BBC Children in Need, partly by subscriptions collected at the door);
- a youth cafe;
- a lunch club for local older residents;
- an adult reading scheme (under contract from the Anytown FE College);
- a homework club (paid for by a grant from the New Opportunities Fund);
- a women's health centre (under contract from the local health authority);
- an IT training project for long-term unemployed people (paid for by the National Lottery Community Fund);

The centre is also hired out for a range of evening activities (Scouts, Brownies, indoor bowls and so on), plus parties, discos and other social functions.

The centre receives a core grant from Anytown Council, and encourages users and local residents to fundraise on its behalf.

On the expenditure side, costs are grouped under the following general headings:
- salaries (including those of a centre manager, a playgroup co-ordinator, a caretaker);
- running costs of the building (rent, rates, heat, light, insurance, post, telephone, photocopier);
- equipment and materials (playgroup equipment, computers, learning materials for the homework club and adult reading scheme);
- publicity, printing and stationery;
- food, drink, kitchen stocks;
- travel and training (including for volunteers).

Management accounts

Management accounts are the regular reports that you receive which update the management committee on the organisation's financial progress in the year so far. They are generally done monthly for larger organisations, or every two to three months for smaller ones. They are based on your annual budget, and assume that your annual budget has also been broken down into monthly or quarterly estimates of income and expenditure – for more information, see *Budgeting and financial planning* on pages 45–47.

Management accounts tend to have two main columns: 'This month', and 'Year to date'. 'This month' looks at income and expenditure for the month in question; 'Year to date' is the total for the year so far. (The accounts may also have the annual total for reference.)

Each main column is then further broken down into three parts: 'Budget', 'Actual' and 'Variance'. 'Budget' is the amount you expect to spend or receive in the month; 'Actual' is the amount you actually spent or received; 'Variance' is the difference between 'Budget' and 'Actual'.

So, for example, here are the May management accounts for Anytown Community Centre.

	This month			Year to date			Annual
	Actual	Budget	Variance	Actual	Budget	Variance	total
Income							
1 Playgroup	410	500	-90	7,260	7,500	-240	16,000
2 Youth cafe	340	400	-60	1,840	2,000	-160	4,800
3 Lunch club	835	780	55	4,020	3,900	120	9,360
4 Reading scheme	0	2,000	-2,000	2,000	4,000	-2,000	8,000
5 Homework club	0	0	0	6,000	6,000	0	12,000
6 Women's health	410	525	-115	2,100	2,800	-700	6,000
7 IT training	6,110	250	5,860	12,970	7,250	5,720	27,000
8 Hire income	780	600	180	3,680	3,000	680	6,000
9 Anytown Council	10,000	10,000	0	10,000	10,000	0	20,000
10 Donations	90	100	-10	440	500	-60	2,500
Total	18,975	15,155	3,820	50,310	46,950	3,360	111,660
Expenditure							
11 Salaries	5,390	5,000	390	26,950	25,000	1,950	60,000
12 Running costs	450	3,250	-2,800	7,640	10,000	-2,360	17,000
13 Equipment	980	1,000	-20	5,040	5,000	40	12,000
14 Publicity	280	250	30	1,340	1,250	90	3,000
15 Food	730	660	70	3,490	3,320	170	8,000
16 Travel	90	160	-70	510	830	-320	2,000
Total	7,920	10,320	-2,400	44,970	45,400	-430	102,000

Note: Under income, all minus figures are worse than budget; under expenditure, all minus figures are better than budget.

Comments

At first sight, the situation looks pretty good. The monthly income is £3,820 better than budgeted; the year to date income is £3,360 better than budgeted. The monthly expenditure is £2,400 better than budget; the year to date expenditure is also under budget, by £430. So, at first glance, all the indicators are positive.

However, you also need to look at management accounts line by line. Having done this, you may conclude that the general summary picture is a fair reflection of the overall trend. Or you may not. In the above example, a careful look at the accounts will give some cause for concern. So, here goes ...

Income

1 **Playgroup**. This is £90 down on the month, and £240 down on the year to date. So, the May figure of −£90 looks to be part of a pattern, rather than just a one-off. Also, we are moving towards the summer months. Does this mean that more or fewer people will attend? In previous years, have hot summer days brought people storming into the playgroup, or have they gone to the park instead? The management committee should be concerned about the playgroup's general performance so far. Does it need to run a publicity campaign, or try to encourage users to bring along other users? Should it have a 'Try four sessions for free' offer, or would this mean more lost income?

   On the positive side, the playgroup is clearly receiving its Children in Need grant on time. The year to date budget is much higher than just five times the monthly budget, which suggests that Children in Need is paying its grant (presumably of £10,000 a year) quarterly or half-yearly in advance, and everything seems to be up to date on that.

2 **Youth cafe**. Like the playgroup, this is behind both on the month and on the year to date. The management committee needs to ask similar questions to those for the playgroup. At this rate, between them the income for the playgroup and youth cafe could be down by over £1,000 by the end of the year.

3 **Lunch club**. This seems to be going well. It is slightly up on the year and on the month. Can we do anything to improve things still further?

4 **Reading scheme**. The overall income for the year is budgeted at £8,000. It seems to be coming in £2,000 chunks, so it looks as if the contract payment from the FE college is paid quarterly. We can infer that an instalment was due in May, but didn't arrive. Is that because the college is late paying or because the community centre was late invoicing? If it is simply that the payment is a week late and will come in early June rather than May, then that is nothing much to worry about. However, if the payment is going to be substantially delayed – or even not come in at all – that's a major issue. All the management committee can do is ask the questions and then decide on action, or not, according to the answers.

5 **Homework club**. Again, this seems all to be paid for by an external grant. Everything is on track. Nothing to worry about.

6 **Women's health**. Another cause for concern. Whereas the playgroup income seems to be a combination of subscriptions paid when people attend, plus an external grant, it is more likely that the women's health centre income is all provided under contract. You can assume this for three reasons:

(a) this kind of health work is often delivered under contract from the local health authority;

(b) a grant is likely to be paid quarterly rather than monthly, and it seems that the women's health project is receiving such income;

(c) it would be a bit odd to have a health centre in a community centre that you had to pay to use.

Obviously, as a management committee member you would need to know (or find out) exactly where the money is coming from. If it is provided under contract it seems either that the contract payments are behind – in which case someone needs to get the invoicing sorted out – or (assuming that the health authority pays according to the number of people using the centre) that the women's health project is not attracting as many people as was hoped – in which case the end of year result is not looking at all promising.

7 **IT training**. Here the situation looks excellent. There's a major surplus on the month, and a major surplus on the year. This may be because the project is genuinely doing really well and lots more people are paying for training sessions than expected. However, it may be because the National Lottery Community Fund grant has come in at the end of May rather than early June. Once again, this is something that you cannot tell from the figures alone; you have to ask questions at the management committee meeting. The role of the management accounts is to alert you to different possibilities as you go through them.

If it is indeed the case that the grant has been paid slightly earlier than anticipated (the most likely scenario), there are problems. Assuming the grant is £6,000 a quarter, which the figures would seem to suggest (as the other budgeted monthly income seems to be £250), if you take £6,000 from the May income and £6,000 from the year-to-date figures, again the IT project is behind budget.

8 **Hire income**. At last, a genuine good news story from these accounts. The income is ahead of budget both in May and for the year as a whole, so May doesn't seem to have been just a one-off good month. The question then becomes: can we do even better? Budgeting and strategic planning are not just about dealing with the bad; they are also about maximising the good.

9 **Anytown Council**. Its grant is on time. Is there any reason to assume that the second instalment will not come in on schedule? If not, no problem.

10 **Donations**. Slightly behind so far, but at this stage the amounts are pretty small anyway. However, it seems that more is expected over the summer (the annual budget is £2,500; the budgeted income so far runs at £100 per month). Is this realistic? If not, there will be a more serious hole in income by the end of the year.

Income summary. The centre appears to have some problems on the income side. On current performance, despite the good results from the lunch club and hire income, it is likely that there will be an overall shortfall of around £2,000–£3,000. This is by no means disastrous, but should be enough to persuade the management committee to look again at how certain activities are run and if there are ways of raising more income from them.

Expenditure

11 **Salaries**. Another cause for concern. They seem to be running at a steady £390 a month worse than budget. This will mean an overall deficit by the year end of nearly £5,000. It looks like a basic budgeting error (sometimes, for example, you can simply forget to allow for salary increases), but one which will have pretty serious consequences. If it continues on its current course, the salary overspend alone will wipe out around half the budgeted annual surplus.

12 **Running costs**. Again, apparently good news that probably isn't. The monthly budget of £3,250 implies that there was a major bill expected (say insurance) that either didn't arrive or wasn't paid. It looks as if the bill was expected to be £2,500–£3,000, given the budget for the month versus the actual, ongoing expenditure for the month. If so, the figures become unrepresentative of the real picture. In reality, running costs are just on budget at best. They are probably worse than budget. Things may well be clearer by the end of June, especially if this infamous bill has finally come in.

13 **Equipment**. This seems to be pretty much on budget. Given expenditure problems elsewhere, you should try to keep a pretty tight lid on this budget.

14 **Publicity**. Again, slightly over budget already. This would mean that spending money on publicity campaigns as suggested above would have to be carefully evaluated. You would need to be pretty certain of getting results.

15 **Food**. Also slightly over budget. Is this because the lunch club is going well? If so, the lunch club figures are not quite as good as they appeared. Do you need to think about charging more for the lunches, because you are not making enough of a surplus on them? But would people pay if you did this?

16 **Travel**. Better than budget. Again, you may need to try to keep it this way.

Expenditure summary. Pretty bleak. If things continue as they are, there will probably be an overspend of at least £7,000.

Overview

Overall, the community centre looks set to make a small loss on the year. While not disastrous, this is a cause for concern, so the management committee can expect to be facing some difficult decisions over the next few months about what is really viable and where the community centre should be putting its energies. Indeed, to be really harsh, quite a few of its activities (such as the playgroup, reading scheme and IT training) are mainly financed by grant income which by its nature is short rather than long-term. What will happen when these grants run out? Somebody could be doing a lot of sponsored runs to make up the shortfall!

When reading management accounts, always remember that they are just a snapshot of an organisation at a particular point in its year. Sometimes, figures that look bad may actually mask a pretty healthy reality; and, as with the community centre example above, vice versa. It may even be that if you took the snapshot two weeks later the situation would look markedly different.

However, management accounts are usually a good guide to what is really going on. Study them carefully and see what you think the underlying message is. And ask whatever questions you need to satisfy yourself that you have a good grasp of the real position. It won't always be as complicated as the example above.

Reading annual accounts

This is a difficult area for a book like this to deal with, because there are different accounting requirements according to a charity's size and set-up (for more information see *Information from the accounting system* on pages 44–45).

Some charities have to divide their income and expenditure into 'restricted' and 'unrestricted' funds. A restricted fund is one where the donor has given money under a certain set of conditions. For example, in the Anytown Community Centre example above, the BBC Children in Need grant for the playgroup would be a restricted fund because it was given specifically for the playgroup. It would be illegal to spend this money on the lunch club, for instance. However, Anytown Council's core grant can be spent on any part of the community centre's activities, and so would be deemed to be an unrestricted fund.

Charity accounts expenditure tends to be classified differently from your management accounts. Whereas Anytown Community Centre's management accounts classify expenditure under functional headings (salaries, equipment, publicity and so on), the annual accounts use more general headings such as direct charitable expenditure, fundraising and publicity costs, management and administration costs, and support costs. It is basically the same information but presented in a different way.

For larger charities (and for charitable companies) there are other key differences between management accounts and annual accounts:

- Management accounts are concerned with money out and money in; annual accounts are concerned about the overall position of the charity at the year end. Annual accounts therefore include non-cash items such as an increase/decrease in the value of charity assets and investments.
- Management accounts focus on when money comes in and when it goes out; annual accounts focus on what is relevant to the year in question. So if you pay rent quarterly in advance and your final rent cheque for the year also covers some of the next year, the annual accounts will make an adjustment to reflect this (pre-payments). Conversely, if your electricity bill is paid after the financial year end but covers some of the months in the final part of that financial year, the accounts will also be adjusted accordingly (accruals).

Therefore, the year end totals on your annual accounts differ from those on your management accounts.

In general, it is best to ask your auditor, independent examiner or treasurer to take you through how your annual accounts work. It's a complicated area, and you need to understand how your charity is affected. Alternatively, read *A Practical Guide to Financial Management for Charities* (for details see page 115).

Either way, don't be put off by figures. It's not that different from reading your own bank statement. Just as you look to see if your car insurance went through your account last month, and make a mental adjustment to the final balance if it didn't, so you look at the management accounts to see what has gone in and gone out and what this means for the organisation as a whole. And then you use this information to help you decide what to do next.

Useful addresses

Charity registration and charity law

Charity Commission

Liverpool: 2nd Floor, 20 Kings Parade, Queens Dock, Liverpool L3 4DQ
London: Harmsworth House, 13–15 Bouverie Street, London EC4Y 8DP
Taunton: Woodfield House, Tangier, Taunton, Somerset TA1 4BL

Enquiry line tel: 0870 333 0123; website: www.charity-commission.gov.uk

The Charity Commission has jurisdiction in England and Wales only.

Organisations in Northern Ireland should contact: The Department of Health & Social Services, Charities Branch, 2 Castle Buildings, Stormont Estate, Belfast BT4 3RA
Tel: 01232 552780

Organisations in Scotland should contact: The Director, The Scottish Charities Office, Crown Office, 25 Chambers Street, Edinburgh EH1 1LA
Tel: 0131 226 2626
For information and advice from the Commission, Inland Revenue and Customs and Excise call 0845 30 20 203. This is a local rate telephone helpline service and is available 08.30 to 18.00, Monday to Friday.

(See page 112 for a selection of Charity Commission publication or visit www.charitycommission.gov.uk for a full list.)

General help and advice

Directory of Social Change, 24 Stephenson Way, London NW1 2DP
website: www.dsc.org.uk
Publications tel: 020 7209 5151; fax: 020 7391 4804; e-mail: books@dsc.org.uk
Courses and conferences tel: 020 7209 4949; fax: 020 7391 4808; e-mail: training @dsc.org.uk

Northern office: Federation House, Hope Street, Liverpool L1 9BW
Tel: 0151 708 0117 (courses and conferences)/0151 708 0136 (research); fax: 0151 708 0139; e-mail: north@dsc.org.uk

The Directory of Social Change is an independent voice for positive social change, set up in 1975 to help voluntary organisations become more effective. We do this by providing practical, challenging and affordable information and training to meet the current, emerging and future needs of the sector. Our main activities include researching and publishing reference guides and handbooks, providing practical training courses, and running conferences and briefing sessions. (See pages 112–115 for publications available from DSC.)

We also organise Charityfair, the largest annual event for the UK voluntary sector, which offers the most extensive selection of training, advice and debate to be found under one roof. It is excellent place for people on a tight budget to get training. Charityfair is normally held in April every year. For details telephone 020 7391 4848.

Local organisations

Councils for Voluntary Service (CVSs) and Rural Community Councils (RCCs)

are registered charities that support local organisations in their area (CVSs tend to work in towns and cities, RCCs in more rural areas).

For information on your local CVS, contact: National Association of Councils for Voluntary Service, Arundel Court, 177 Arundel Street, Sheffield S1 2NU
Tel: 0114 278 6636

For information on your nearest RCC, contact: Action with Communities in Rural England (ACRE), Somerford Court, Somerford Road, Cirencester, Glos GL7 1TW
Tel: 01285 653477

National organisations

At the national level the National Councils for Voluntary Service also provide help and advice. Contact:

In England: National Council for Voluntary Organisations, Regent's Wharf, 8 All Saints Street, London N1 9RL
Tel: 020 7713 6161; website: www.ncvo-vol.org.uk; e-mail: ncvo@ncvo-vol. org.uk
HelpDesk tel: 0800 2 798 798; e-mail: helpdesk @ncvo-vol.org.uk

In Northern Ireland: Northern Ireland Council for Voluntary Action, 61 Duncairn Gardens, Belfast BT15 2GB
Tel: 028 9087 7777; website: www.nicva.org

In Scotland: Scottish Council for Voluntary Organisations, 18–19 Claremont Crescent, Edinburgh EH7 4QD
Tel: 0131 556 3882; fax: 0131 556 0279; website: www.scvo.org.uk

In Wales: Wales Council for Voluntary Action, Baltic House, Mount Stuart Square, Cardiff CF10 5FH
Tel: 029 2043 1700; fax: 029 2043 1701; website: www.wcva.org.uk

Equal opportunities

Commission for Racial Equality, Elliott House, 10–12 Allington Street, London SW1E 5EH
Tel: 020 7828 7022; fax: 020 7630 7605; website: www.cre.gov.uk

Equal Opportunities Commission, Arndale House, Arndale Centre, Manchester M4 3EQ
Tel: 0161 833 9244; fax: 0161 838 8312; website: www.eoc.org.uk; e-mail: info@eoc.org.uk

Fundraising

For codes of practice on fundraising, contact:

Institute of Fundraising, Market Towers, 1 Nine Elms Lane, London SW8 5NQ
Tel: 020 7627 3436; website: www.institute-of-fundraising.org.uk

Lotteries and gaming

For information about raffles, lotteries and other forms of gaming activity, contact:

Gaming Board for Great Britain, 168–173 High Holborn, London WC1V 7AA
Tel 020 7306 6200; website: www.gbgb.org.uk

Tax and giving

For information and advice about the taxation of charities, contact:

For England, Wales and Northern Ireland: Inland Revenue FICO, St John's House, Merton Road, Bootle, Merseyside L69 9BB
Tel: 0151 472 6000

For Scotland: FICO, Trinity Park House, South Trinity Road, Edinburgh EH5 3SD
Tel: 0131 552 6255

For information about VAT, contact Customs & Excise (look in your phone book under 'Customs & Excise')

For information about tax-effective giving, contact:

Charities Aid Foundation, King's Hill, West Malling, Kent ME19 4TA
Tel: 01732 520000; fax: 01732 520001; website: www.cafonline.org; e-mail: enquiries@caf.charitynet.org

Volunteering

For advice and information on the law and best practice in volunteering, contact:

National Centre for Volunteering, Regent's Wharf, 8 All Saints Street, London N1 9RL
Tel: 020 7520 8900; website: www.volunteering.org.uk; e-mail: information@ thecentre.org.uk

Major sources of funding

Individuals are by far the biggest givers to charity, whether through legacies, regular donations or one-off gifts. In addition, grant-making trusts and foundations in the UK give about £2,000 million annually to charities, while UK companies give around £250 million a year in cash donations (see page 113 for a list of fundraising directories that should help you to approach these organisations). However, the largest single source of funds for voluntary organisations, and for arts, sports and heritage projects, is the National Lottery, launched in 1994. It is owned and operated under licence until 2009 by Camelot plc.

National Lottery Distribution Boards

In the new licence period (2002–09), after operating expenses, prize money and tax, 28.5% of the total income from lottery games and scratch cards is passed to the National Lottery Distribution Fund to be distributed to good causes. This Fund in turn passes the money to five Distribution Boards:

- The Community Fund (formerly known as the National Lottery Charities Board, or NLCB)
- The Arts Councils in England, Scotland, Wales and Northern Ireland
- The Sports Councils in the same four countries
- The Heritage Lottery Fund
- The New Opportunities Fund

The National Lottery now has a central enquiry line and website:
Tel. 0845 275 0000; textphone: 0845 275 0022; website: www.lotterygoodcauses. org.uk

The Community Fund

This Fund aims to 'help meet the needs of those at greatest disadvantage in society, and to improve the quality of life in the community'.

Contact: Community Fund, St Vincent House, 16 Suffolk Street, London SW1Y 4NL
Tel: 020 7747 5299/application packs 0845 791 9191; website: www.community-fund.org.uk

Arts

Arts grants are covered by the Arts Councils of England, Scotland, Wales and Northern Ireland. Almost any type of organisation may apply for a grant.

In March 2001 the Arts Council of England announced plans to unite with the 10 Regional Arts Boards (RABs) to create a single funding and development organisation for all the arts in all parts of England. The new arrangements were due to come into effect from April 2002.

For England, contact: The Arts Council of England, 14 Great Peter Street, London SW1P 3NQ
Tel: 020 7973 6517; fax: 020 7973 6590; website: www.artscouncil.org.uk/ funding; e-mail: enquiries@artscouncil.org.uk

For Wales, contact: The Arts Council of Wales, Holst House, 9 Museum Place, Cardiff, CF1 3NX
Tel: 029 2037 6500; fax: 029 2022 1447; website: www.ccc-acw.org.uk; e-mail: information@ccc-acw.org.uk

For Scotland, contact: The Scottish Arts Council, 12 Manor Place, Edinburgh EH3 7DD
Tel: 0131 226 6051; fax: 0131 225 9833; website: www.sac.org.uk; e-mail: help.desk.sac@artsfb.org.uk

For Northern Ireland, contact: The Arts Council of Northern Ireland, MacNeice House, 77 Malone Road, Belfast BT9 6AQ
Tel: 028 9038 5200; fax: 028 9066 1715; website: www.artscouncil-ni.org; e-mail: publicaffairs@artscouncil-ni.org

Sports

As with the Arts Councils, each of the national Sports Council has its own independent budget. Money is given not only to elite sportspeople but also, through the Community Projects Fund, for sport as a means of community development.

For England, contact: Sport England Lottery Fund, Community Projects Capital Fund, PO Box 649, London WC1H 0QS
Lottery line tel: 0845 7 649 649; website: english.sports.gov.uk/lottery

For Wales, contact: Sports Council for Wales, Sophia Gardens, Cardiff, CF11 9SW
Tel: 029 2030 0500; website: www.sports-council-wales.co.uk

For Scotland, contact: Sport Scotland, Caledonia House, South Gyle, Edinburgh EH12 9DQ
Tel: 0131 339 9000; website: www.sportscotland.org.uk

For Northern Ireland, contact: Lottery Fund, Sports Council for Northern Ireland, House of Sport, Upper Malone Road, Belfast BT9 5LA
Tel: 028 9038 2222; website: www.sportni.org

Heritage

The Heritage Lottery Fund makes available minimum grants of £10,000, for a range of activities connected with museums, libraries and the national heritage generally (including transport and maritime heritage). Separate country committees are now expected to make decisions on grants of less than £1 million.

Contact: Heritage Lottery Fund, 7 Holbein Place, London SW1W 8NR
Tel: 020 7591 6000; fax: 020 7591 6001; website: www.hlf.org.uk; e-mail: enquire@hlf.org.uk

The New Opportunities Fund

The Fund distributes Lottery money to government-determined initiatives in the areas of health, education and the environment. These include healthy living centres, out-of-school-hours childcare, training in information and communications technology, and adult learning.

Contact: New Opportunities Fund, Heron House, 322 High Holborn, London WC1V 7PW
Tel: 0845 000 0120; website: www.nof.org.uk; e-mail: general.enquiries@nof.org.uk

Awards for All

This is the small grants programme in England and Scotland. The Arts, Charity, Heritage and Sports Distributors make grants in the range of £500–£5,000 to small charities and community groups with an annual income of less than £15,000. The bulk of the funding is for Community Fund projects.

Contact: Awards for All
Tel: 0845 600 2040; website: www.awardsforall.org.uk

Government funding

Central government departments and agencies give funding to voluntary organisations if their work falls within certain areas of government policy. Different departments fund various different programmes, which are open to annual applications, although the criteria for these may change from year to year. Voluntary and community groups are advised to check the relevant websites to see which programmes are currently operating.

In the 2000/01 financial year the following departments ran programmes specifically for voluntary organisations:

Department of Culture, Media and Sport (DCMS), 2–6 Cockspur Street, London SW1Y 5DH
Tel: 020 7211 6000; fax: 020 7211 6032; website: www.culture.gov.uk; e-mail: enquiries@culture.gov.uk

Department of Health, Richmond House, 79 Whitehall, London SW1A 2NS
Tel: 020 7210 3000; fax: 020 7210 5523; website: www.doh.gov.uk

Home Office, 50 Queen Anne's Gate, London SW1H 9AT
Tel: 020 7273 4000; fax: 020 7273 2190; website: www.homeoffice.gov.uk

Programmes were also run by the former Department for Education and Employment and the former Department of the Environment, Transport and the Regions, which were both reorganised in June 2001. At the time of going to press, the contact details of the new departments were as follows:

Department for Education and Skills
website: www.dfes.gov.uk

Department for Work and Pensions
website: www.dwp.gov.uk

Department for the Environment, Food and Rural Affairs
website: www.defra.gov.uk

Department for Transport, Local Government and the Regions
website: www.dtlr.gov.uk

Publications

Charity Commission publications

The Charity Commission produces a range of free leaflets. The most generally useful free publications include:

CC3 – Responsibilities of Charity Trustees

CC7 – Ex Gratia Payments by Charities

CC8 – Internal Financial Controls for Charities

CC9 – Political Activities and Campaigning by Charities

CC9a – Political Activities and Campaigning by Local Community Charities

CC11 – Payment of Charity Trustees

CC12 – Managing Financial Difficulties and Insolvency in Charities

CC14 – Investment of Charitable Funds

CC14a – Depositing Charity Cash

CC18 – Use of Church Halls for Village Hall and Other Charitable Purposes

CC19 – Charities' Reserves

CC20 – Charities and Fund-raising

CC21 – Registering as a Charity

CC22 – Choosing and Preparing a Governing Document

CC24 – Users on Board: beneficiaries who become trustees

CC27 – Providing Alcohol on Charity Premises

CC35 – Charities and Trading

CC49 – Charities and Insurance

CC60 – The Hallmarks of a Well-run Charity

CC61 – Charity Accounts 2001: the framework

GD1 – Model Memorandum and Articles of Association for a Charitable Company

GD2 – Model Declaration of Trust for a Charitable Trust

GD3 – Model Constitution for a Charitable Unincorporated Association

Also available:
A Guide to the Charities Acts 1992 and 1993
Charity Commission video – It's a Question of Trust

(See page 106 for contact details for the Charity Commission.)

Publications available from DSC

The following is a selection of publications available from the Directory of Social Change (DSC), the leading publisher and provider of training for the voluntary sector. Prices were correct at the time of writing, but may be subject to change. Please also note that new editions of our directories are usually published every two years. (See page 106 for contact details to request a complete list of current publications.)

Fundraising directories and CD-ROMs

There are thousands of trusts and foundations in the UK which give grants to charities and other voluntary organisations. However, their funding criteria differ – some only give money for certain specified causes; some only give in certain geographic areas – as does the information they require from applicants. To help you identify those trusts who may fund your particular cause, the following directories give detailed information, including independent commentary, on the largest UK trusts (respectively, the top 300; the next 700; and the next 400):

A Guide to the Major Trusts, volume 1, DSC, £20.95
A Guide to the Major Trusts, volume 2, DSC, £20.95
A Guide to the Major Trusts, volume 3, DSC, £17.95

Or you can find less detailed information, on 2,500 trusts, in:

The Directory of Grant Making Trusts, published in association with Charities Aid Foundation 2003, £80

Information and commentary on trusts that give in specific areas of England can be found in one of the four volumes of *A Guide to Local Trusts*, covering Greater London, the Midlands, the North and the South of England, respectively (DSC, £17.95 each)

For information on Scotland, turn to:

The Guide to Scottish Trusts, DSC 2002, £16.95

For information on Wales, turn to:

The Welsh Funding Guide, DSC forthcoming 2003, c.£16.95

All our trusts information, covering over 4,000 trusts, is also available on CD-ROM (DSC, £135 including VAT) or via our subscription website *www.trustfunding.org.uk*

The Grant-making Trusts CD-ROM, DSC, £129.25 (including VAT)

If you are trying to raise money or other support from the corporate sector, you can refer to either a directory or a CD:

The Guide to UK Company Giving, DSC, £25
The CD-ROM Company Giving Guide, DSC, £58.75 (including VAT)

Those who are fundraising for schools can turn to:

The Schools Funding Guide, Nicola Eastwood, Anne Mountfield and Louise Walker, DSC 2001, £16.95

Fundraising handbooks

A popular title that provides detailed practical advice on all aspects of fundraising for charity is:

The Complete Fundraising Handbook, 4th edition, Nina Botting and Michael Norton, DSC 2001, £16.95

If you want information on how to approach funders, read the following:

Finding Company Sponsors for Good Causes, Chris Wells, DSC 2000, £9.95
Fundraising from Grant-making Trusts and Foundations, Karen Gilchrist and Margo Horsley, DSC 2000, £10.95

To help you put together effective applications for support, turn to:

Writing Better Fundraising Applications, 3rd edition, Michael Norton and Mike Eastwood, DSC 2002, £14.95

Once you have secured your donors, advice on how to develop your links with them is given in:

Looking after your Donors, Karen Gilchrist, DSC 2000, £10.95

Details of how to plan and organise different types of fundraising events are provided by these books:

Organising Special Events for Fundraising and Campaigning, John F. Gray and Stephen Elsden, DSC 2000, £10.95
Tried and Tested Ideas for Local Fundraising Events, 3rd edition, Sarah Passingham, DSC 2003, £14.95

Management

The standard guide for managers of small and medium-sized voluntary organisations is:

Just About Managing?, 3rd edition, Sandy Adirondack, London Voluntary Service Council 1998, £18.95

A practical approach to business planning in the voluntary sector is provided by:

The Complete Guide to Business and Strategic Planning for Voluntary Organisations, Alan Lawrie, 2nd edition, DSC 2001, £12.50

Aspects of people-management are covered in:

Essential Volunteer Management, 2nd edition, Steve McCurley and Rick Lynch, DSC 1998, £14.95
The Health & Safety Handbook for Voluntary & Community Organisations, Al Hinde and Charlie Kavanagh, edited by Jill Barlow, 2nd edition, DSC/Liverpool Occupational Health Partnership 2001, £12.50

Recruiting Volunteers, Fraser Dyer & Ursula Jost, DSC 2002, £10.95

Communication

Every voluntary organisation needs to put its message across effectively. The following titles all provide you with helpful, practical advice on this:

The Campaigning Handbook, Mark Lattimer, 2nd edition, DSC 2000, £15.95
Promoting Your Cause, Karen Gilchrist, DSC 2002, £10.95
How to Produce Inspiring Annual Reports: a guide for voluntary, arts and campaigning organisations, Ken Burnett and Karin Weatherup, DSC 2000, £12.50

Finance

Don't let figures frighten you. If you have been asked to be treasurer of a voluntary group, or simply want a good grounding in how charity finances work, try:

The Charity Treasurer's Handbook, Gareth Morgan, DSC 2002, £9.95

If you are looking for information on more specific financial areas, these two books will guide you through what you need to know:

A Practical Guide to Charity Accounting, Kate Sayer, DSC 2003, £14.95
A Practical Guide to Financial Management for Charities, 2nd edition, Kate Sayer, DSC 2002, £14.95
A Practical Guide to VAT for Charities and Voluntary Organisations, 2nd edition, Kate Sayer, DSC 2001, £12.95

Law

Our key introductory guide to what is a charity, and what constitutes charitable activity, is:

Charitable Status, Andrew Phillips, DSC 2003, £16.95

You can find definitive information on the law as it affects charities, community groups and other voluntary organisations in:

The Voluntary Sector Legal Handbook, 2nd edition, Sandy Adirondack and James Sinclair Taylor, DSC 2001, £42 for voluntary organisations/£60 for others

Details of specific topics are provided in:

Data Protection for Voluntary Organisations, 2nd edition, Paul Ticher, DSC 2003, £14.95
The Minute Taker's Handbook, Lee Comer and Paul Ticher, DSC 2002, £9.95